Legal Notice:

While all attempts have been made to verify information provided in this publication, neither the Author nor the Publisher assumes any responsibility for errors, omissions, or contrary interpretation of the subject matter herein.

This publication is not intended for use as a source of legal or accounting advice. The Publisher wants to stress that the information contained herein may be subject to varying state and/or local laws or regulations. All users are advised to retain competent counsel to determine what state and/or local laws or regulations may apply to the user's particular business.

The purchaser or reader of this publication assumes responsibility for the use of these materials and information. Adherence to all applicable laws and regulations, federal, state, and local, governing professional licensing, business practices, advertising, and all other aspects of doing business in the United States or any other jurisdiction is the sole responsibility of the purchaser or reader.

The Author and Publisher assume no responsibility or liability whatsoever on behalf of any purchaser or reader of these materials. Any perceived slights of specific people or organizations are unintentional.

SECRETS of Online PERSUASION

Captivating the Hearts, Minds and Pocketbooks of Thousands Using Blogs, Podcasts and other New Media Marketing Tools

JOHN-PAUL & DEBORAH MICEK

Morgan James Publishing • NEW YORK

SECRETS of Online PERSUASION

Copyright ©2006 RPM Success Group® Inc. / John-Paul and Deborah Cole Micek

Version 2.0 All rights reserved.

No part of this publication may be reproduced or transmitted in any form or by any means, mechanical or electronic, including photocopying and recording, or by any information storage and retrieval system, without permission in writing from the publisher.

Library of Congress Cataloging in-Publication Data:

Micek, Deborah and John-Paul

SECRETS of Online PERSUASION: Captivating the Hearts, Minds and Pocketbooks of Thousands Using Blogs, Podcasts & Other New Media Marketing Tools

p. cm.

ISBN 1-60037-029-2

1. Marketing 2. Business Blogging 3. Small Business Development

Printed and bound in the United States of America.

Published by:

MORGAN · JAMES™
THE ENTREPRENEURIAL PUBLISHER
www.morganjamespublishing.com

Morgan James Publishing, LLC
1225 Franklin Ave Ste 32
Garden City, NY 11530-1693
Toll Free 800-485-4943
www.MorganJamesPublishing.com

Information on use permissions and/or TeleCourse details should be addressed to:

RPM Success Group® Inc
Toll Free (888) 334-8151
International: 00+1+808+237+1008
Email: support@RPMsuccess.com
http://www.RPMsuccess.com

Habitat for Humanity®
Peninsula
Building Partner

» Dedication

This book is dedicated to Stephen Pierce, our coach, mentor and brother, who inspired us to listen carefully to our market, take immediate action on our ideas, innovate until our ideas turned into a profitable venture and persist until we saw our dreams turn into reality.

This book was created for all the innovators and visionaries who know how to turn a concept into an idea and an idea into a profitable business that creates opportunities for others to succeed – and to those who know the importance of doing it sooner rather than later.

~ Deborah Cole Micek and John-Paul Micek

The basic principle of turning ideas into big money is to seize every money-building idea and work with it until the idea fits your purpose, decide on the steps needed to make it work, and then proceed to do it as soon as possible.

~ Duane Newcomb

»What people are saying about Coach Deborah and John Paul's BLOG Interactive 360™ Coaching Programs

I liked how specific and logical everything is laid out in your course. It's not just vague conceptual ideas about how business blogging should be. Instead, it's, "Here's the 1,2,3,4,5 of this strategy" and then you give us the 1-2-3-4-5 coaching steps on how to apply it. That is so helpful.

- Catherine Bruns
www.coachbalance.com

I work with Web stuff all the time – and you gave an UNBELIEVABLE amount of practical information in this course! I will listen to this over and over again! You shared SO many strategies that I can immediately apply to market my business blog.

~ Kevin Finneran
'Synergy' worldwide distributor

X | WHAT PEOPLE ARE SAYING

I enjoyed your course so much. Before this, ***I was a techno-phobe.*** *When I first heard of blogging I thought, "Wow that sounds like a cute word." I didn't even know what it was. But after taking your course, I created my first blog!*

Business blogging is so simple *– anybody can do it with the step-by-step instructions you give. You two are like walking encyclopedias of knowledge. You're the perfect team for busy business owners. I am SO glad I took this course.*

~ Beth Borray
Red Peony Consulting

I spent over $1,300 that I didn't need to trying to do things on my own. Now, with the tips and strategies you've shown me I've tripled the traffic to my site and grown my subscriber list by over 400%!

I wish I got your book sooner!

~ John Allen Mollenhauer
www.mytrainer.com

Excellent instructions with all the ***workbooks, audio recordings and videos*** *you created for us! It's superb. Thank you so much. You two are a wonderful team – you each have a different style and it blends so beautifully that it makes all the difference in the world.*

~ Julie Rose
Roselight Gardens

What People are Saying | XI

I saw my Web site visitors double almost overnight after I started business blogging! And once I added podcasting to my business blog, I went from less than 1,000 visitors to more than 5,000 visitors in just two weeks!

This is an absolutely fantastic course. It has totally transformed how I write anything, from e-mail, to blogs, to Web site copy.

~ Penny Haynes
Encouraging Audio Productions

The BLOG Interactive 360™ Course was an exceptional learning experience. Deborah & John Paul Micek are experts in their knowledge and understanding in the application of blogs, RSS, and Podcasting for business growth in just about any type of industry or profession.

Even with my extensive experience in Web site development I learned a great deal from this course. I substantially increased my understanding, application, and results with marketing strategies, keyword selection/positioning, search engine marketing, social networking, and much more.

I witnessed first hand how easy the course made it for students to apply these techniques and get bottom line results through their blogs.

~ Keith Troup
www.idmstudios.com

4 Days after creating my blogs, 2 major media outlets called me for an interview on the same day!

One night after following your advice, I set up 3 different blogs, to start building some traffic to one of my Web sites.

Now, it could be a "coincidence" but honest to God, just 4 days later, **in the very same day**, I heard from both **CNN Money** and *The Wall Street Journal*.

XII | WHAT PEOPLE ARE SAYING

The fact that I put all these blogs out there must have had something to do with it. To hear from two of the biggest media outlets on the SAME day, so soon after I had created my blogs as you instructed is HUGE! My blogs certainly helped them find me.

Naturally, that drove significant traffic to my site, and I've gotten a lot of business from it since! Now I'm linked from the CNN Money site back to my SixElements.com site, which is a big help with search engines!

Right after the CNN story came out, I started getting a lot of inquiries from all across North America for home stagers, which is one of the things I do, so now I've got this huge referral business going as I'm sending referrals to graduates of my home staging training program – so a lot of business results came out of my blogging efforts, and following your advice in fast order – this is fabulous!

Then, those media stories got picked up on a lot of other Web sites and news sites, and carried by other newspapers, so news continues to spread about my business!

It was so funny because anytime the phone rang that day, we joked, "Hey, this must be ABC calling!"

~ Debra Gould
The Staging Diva™

President, Six Elements Inc.
Toronto, Canada

http://www.stagingdiva.com
http://www.sixelements.com

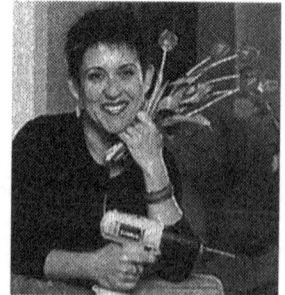

» Contents

FOREWORD by Dave Lakhani, author of XXI
Persuasion: The Art of Getting What you Want

INTRODUCTION　　　　　　　　　　XXV

SECTION I
Mastering the New Media Marketplace

1 | CHAPTER 1. *The New Media Revolution:* Cash in with the cultural tsunami sweeping the international marketplace

15 | CHAPTER 2. *The New Media Marketplace:* How to work with (and win in) the New Media culture

29 | CHAPTER 3. *The New Media Consumer:* What makes the New Media consumer tick (and how rubbing people the wrong way can torpedo your best efforts)

43 | CHAPTER 4. *Your New Media Toolbox:* It's Tool Time! Meet the New Media Tools that work hard for you… 24/7

61 | CHAPTER 5. *The New Media Marketing Mindset:* Innovative thinking that trumps technology every time

SECTION II
BUSINESS BLOGGING SECRETS REVEALED!

77 | CHAPTER 6. *Blogging for your business is NOT what you think*

85 | CHAPTER 6.5. *Pulling back the curtain to meet the Wizard of Blogs*

99 | CHAPTER 7. *Planning for long term success*

113 | CHAPTER 8. *Make your blogging fast, easy and fun with the best software for your unique needs*

125 | CHAPTER 9. *Content that creates raving fans*

141 | CHAPTER 9.5. *Laying out the spider bait*

163 | CHAPTER 10. *Boosting the performance on your blog*

SECTION III
INFLUENCE & PERSUASION SECRETS REVEALED!

179 | CHAPTER 11. *Tribal Marketing: the secret strategy for high leverage to influence your target audience*

197 | CHAPTER 12. *Influencing the Influencers… winning through personal persuasion!*

227 | CHAPTER 13. *The Art and Science of Effectively Persuading Your Target Audience and the Masses*

243 | CHAPTER 14. *Ten Commandments of Marketing with the New Media* *(to avoid the wrath of the marketplace)*

SECTION IV
TAKE ACTION!

255 | CHAPTER 15. *Podcasting for Profit*

273 | CHAPTER 16. *iBuzz: Creative ways to use Podcasts and other Multimedia Tools for Runaway Word-of-Mouth Marketing Impact*

275 | CHAPTER 17. *iBrand: The Fingerprint of Emotion (verses the smudge of mass media)*

277 | CHAPTER 18. *iConnect: The Handshake Heard Around the World*

279 | CHAPTER 19. *iProfit: The 360º System for New Media Marketing*

283 | CHAPTER 20. *Final words from your Coaches on using New Media*

ACKNOWLEDGEMENTS	291
MEET YOUR AUTHORS AND COACHES	295
ADDITIONAL RESOURCES	301

» Foreword

Friends; families; relationships; cults; tribes ...

They all have one thing in common.

Persuasion.

In today's rapidly changing marketplace, we all hope to deepen our relationships with people and create a swarm of hungry customers. Or, as the Miceks so aptly demonstrate, we should be creating tribes.

Tribes are unified groups bound together by tradition, common thought, shared beliefs, and a common interpretation of the symbols around them including marketing and advertising messages. They come together for a common purpose – to support and to receive support from one another. They are highly influenced by the other members of the tribe and they exert great influence in the tribe.

But how do you create such a tribe – a connected community that pulls together to support each other and you?

The best answer today is by using social media to build your tribe online. Borders, time, and distance have been erased allowing your customers to communicate nearly as instantly as they experience something – and they do. *Secrets of Online Persuasion* leads you step-by-step through the process of connecting with others like you and attracting them to you to build a thriving tribe. It teaches you very specific processes of education – two-way interactive communication through multiple channels that allows you to influence members of the tribe.

In today's instantly connected economy, tribes communicate faster and better than ever before. They sit in the theater and tell their friends via text messaging during the movie not to waste their money, not on the movie or the new restaurant they tried before the show.

The tribe speaks, the movie dies, and so does the restaurant because the word spreads in minutes – not days, weeks, months, or years – minutes.

The same thing happens in every business in the world every day. Consumers speak, trends start, businesses grow – or they are damned – with the click of a mouse or the push of a send button.

In order to succeed today, you must not only understand what your consumers want, but how they find that information, validate it, and make decisions.

This book makes that process predictable, profitable, and easy.

When I wrote my #1 best-selling book, *Persuasion: The Art of Getting What You Want*, I included one chapter on influencing online. This book doesn't just blow that chapter out of the water, it expands on the major premise of the chapter in ways I should have, but never would have. And, the reason I wouldn't have is quite simple. Deborah and John-Paul live and breathe online influence every day. They are in the trenches developing, testing, and implementing for their clients, and this book is filled with the result of that labor. It is a playbook for any businessperson who is serious about attracting, building a relationship, and influencing the most valuable customers in the market today – all the while gently leading them, no, compelling them to join, to take part, to participate.

Loyalty is dead. It harks back to a construct where people are forced through limitation, availability, and lack of information to stay connected with a brand. That kind of experience no longer exists precisely because of the Internet. Tribethink and Tribespeak now rules the day.

Tribal relationships are the customer loyalty of our age and you are about to embark on the best education you can get on exactly how to turn your customers, your fans, your following, into a connected, supportive community with you at the center. And, you are going to profit from it for decades to come.

Don't just read this book; take action; study the book; implement the ideas and you'll profit immediately.

By reading this book and taking action, you're joining a tribe of enlightened marketers, marketers who'll share with you, educate you, and learn from you. You are now part of a living, breathing, marketing organism that is growing and changing. You hold in your hands the tools to succeed.

Welcome to the tribe of online persuaders.

Read on to find out what to do next.

DAVE LAKHANI

author of *Persuasion: The Art of Getting What You Want*

www.boldapproach.com

Man's mind, once stretched to a new idea,

never goes back to its original dimensions.

~ Oliver Wendell Holmes

»Introduction

On September 8, 2004, the tidal wave of transformation came crashing in.

A power shift that had been simmering below the surface for years finally boiled over into simultaneous national recognition.

Like Goliath being slain with a lowly slingshot, the mass media came to the undeniable realization that they were no longer solely in control of information.

A tidal wave of information and transformation swept over the online marketplace and worldwide culture simultaneously.

Within 30 minutes of the infamous "60 Minutes II" TV broadcast ending, bloggers were already digging into the facts and questioning the validity of the documents that had just been presented by the 42-year broadcast veteran Dan Rather. In less than one week, CBS was forced to admit it could "no longer vouch for the memos." And just weeks after the United States Presidential election, Rather announced his retirement and the blogosphere won another victory.

That one event not only created a tidal surge of public awareness of blogging and New Media. It made Deborah and I realize that this tremendous power of the New Media could be harnessed for business as well as for politics.

Maybe it was our recent move from New Jersey to Hawaii, and the initial isolation that we were still feeling. Or maybe it was the utter frustration of failing to make something work on the Internet after starting, growing and selling three very successful off-line businesses.

Quite possibly it was a combination of those two things along with a passion for political undercurrents in the US that made us keenly aware of what was going on worldwide. Whatever it was with that one event, something clicked.

It was then we saw there was a way to integrate our education and experience in psychology, selling, and business ownership into the online world. We saw that there finally was a way to flatten the marketplace and level the playing field. A new virtual playing field that would allow professionals and businesses of all sizes to attract, interact with, and retain a highly targeted audience online.

On that sunny, summer afternoon in 2004, we didn't yet know how the power of the New Media could be harnessed for business. But we knew if it could be done for politics, it could be done for business.

At that point, we'd merely been dabbling with business blogging. We were using it as a white hat search engine optimization strategy to garner top search engine positioning. And as a tool to archive, syndicate, and deliver our newspaper and magazine articles to our clients and grow our prospect list.

Now, after two years of research, over 4,200 hours of testing, and fine tuning through our consulting and coaching with business owners around the world -- we've developed a completely integrated system that allows professionals and business owners to harness the power of the New Media marketplace for more clients, more sales, and more profits.

What you hold in your hands is the roadmap to a simple system. A system that will deliver more buzz, more branding, more connections, and more profits from the online marketplace than you ever thought possible. Whether you have a local business with a geographically limited reach, or a company that does business around the world -- it works.

By the time you finish this book, you will not only understand what the New Media is, and how this tsunami of information and cultural transformation is redefining the marketplace of the new millennium; you'll also clearly see what you need to do in order to harness its power and put it to work for you and your business.

Your success starts with forgetting everything you've heard about New Media

If you've been listening to how the mass (so-called "mainstream") media is defining New Media ... forget everything you've heard. They don't have a clue on what it is. Never mind tell you how to harness its power for your business. And unfortunately, it's the same story with most advertising firms and marketing gurus.

It's really amazing how "out to lunch" the mass media is. Their thinking is like sheltered Victorian-era men and women driving Model-Ts who, when they see an F-18 fighter jet fly by overhead, they shudder in fear calling the flight "demonic."

They see bloggers and the New Media in extremes. They see either a bunch of political hacks using the Internet to spread "undocumented" news stories, or a bunch of horny teens using some cool new software.

Similar to marketing gurus and big advertising companies, the Mainstream media mistakenly sees the "technology" as the New Media. As you eagerly devour this book, you'll learn why both views are flawed.

The New Media is not simply blogs, Podcasts, social networks, and other new technologies. It's an interlaced matrix of interactive tools that has customer control and participation as its inexhaustible power supply.

Psychology, participation, and the filling of deep-seated human needs are powering the New Media marketplace. And this **human element** is what's making this is an unstoppable trend, *not the technology*.

The process of successfully marketing and selling is being transformed right before our eyes. It's the proactive businessperson who will see the New Media tidal wave sweeping through the marketplace. And it's the women and men with that contextual understanding that will master the marketplace of the new millennium.

Is New Media going to transform the marketplace with a cataclysmic event, or with a whisper? The answer is already right before our very eyes.

Grab your surfboard and prepare yourself to ride this tidal wave of transformation to a lead position in your niche.

It's time to roll!

Are you ready?

YOURS IN PERSUASION AND PROFITS,

Deborah Cole and John Paul Micek
The World's Premiere New Media Marketing Coaches
C.P.B.A., C.P.V.A. (Certified Professional Behavior and Values Analyst)

Section I

»Mastering the New Media Marketplace

The New Media Revolution

chapter one

>> **The tidal wave of cultural transformation is not coming. It has already hit.**

"They are the gatekeepers. They are guarding all the doors and they are holding all the keys, which means that sooner or later someone is going to have to fight them.

I won't lie to you Neo. Every single man or woman who has stood their ground, everyone who has fought an agent has died. But where they have failed, you will succeed.

I've seen an agent punch through a concrete wall; men have emptied entire clips at them and hit nothing but air. Yet their strength and their power is still based in a world that is built on rules. Because of that they will never be as strong or as fast as you can be."

– *Morpheus to Neo in the movie, The Matrix*

Most people are missing it, and that's good ... for you. Because now, with the help of what we'll be sharing with you in this book, you'll see opportunities where your competitors and peers feel confusion and frustration.

What's the mistake? What are people missing? It's the tidal wave of cultural transformation that's sweeping the modern marketplace – a revolution that's happening offline, online, and everywhere in between.

It's easy to miss. Since this reformation of the marketplace is being powered by the New Media, it looks like it's all about technology. And that intimidates most people. But don't allow yourself to be fooled. It's not about the Internet, blogs, iPods, or any other cool new tool on its own.

People, participation and persuasion are generating the Revolution.

That's so important to your business success in the marketplace of the new millennium that it bears repeating. The New Media Revolution is about people, participation, and persuasion.

Grasp this one concept and you'll quickly leapfrog your competitors to lead your niche in marketing, buzz, and branding.

As Seth Godin first forecasted in his 1999 book *Permission Marketing*, traditional advertising and marketing through interruption is dead. Today, despite the companies large and small who still blindly stumble along, following habitual patterns of the past, the new millennium consumer has proved Seth's forecast to be true.

Will you follow in those same old footsteps until the reality of failure hits you? Or will you ignore the lie that others are telling themselves and profit from this exciting new marketplace?

The Lie We've All Been Living

When looking at what's happening in the marketplace, especially New Media, many people, including industry experts and experienced consultants, are focused on the "new" technologies of the New Media. Many more are caught up with a focus on the "media" of blogs, Podcasts, social networks, and other New Media tools.

Keep in mind, it's not about the newness of technology and tools. The cultural transformation we're experiencing is certainly enabled by New Media. Yet if you're going to quickly adapt and profit in this new marketplace, it's critical to understand that this Revolution is a much deeper, cultural event. It's about returning to what drives us as human beings.

This is easy to see when we look at 8,000 years of recorded history. What's happened to marketing and communications over the last 80 years is an anomaly. A departure from what's natural for human beings.

From the birth of Christ, through the golden age of Islam at the end of the first millennium, the creation of the Gutenberg press in 1440, to the American Revolution in 1776 and beyond – the universal hunger has always been for freedom, connection, and participation. With each transformational period in history, people have been drawn to what empowers them and enhances what makes human beings human.

The latest interruption to that drive for freedom, connection, and participation began in the 1920s with the emergence of the first radio and television stations. It was harmless enough at first. Even helpful to bring people together as families gathered together in the living room to watch *I Love Lucy*.

But from the very start, the mindset of the Industrial Revolution was intertwined with mass media. Mass production and mass distribution permeated every area of the marketplace, and for nearly three quarters of a century that methodology continued to expand like a cancerous growth throughout mass media.

The lie spread (that this one-way channel is THE way to connect with people) and became so much a part of our lives that we didn't even stop to see it for what it really was.

THEN, LIKE MANY TIMES BEFORE IN HISTORY, THE REVOLUTION BEGAN.

The Ripples That Became A Tsunami

Like a series of earthquakes occurring in the middle of the ocean, deep on the sea floor, it went mostly unnoticed.

- The emergence of popular talk radio in 1989.
- The information superhighway of the Internet in the early 1990s.
- Lightning-fast viral communication through online social networks and blogs in the early years of the new millennium.
- Tools and media that put the customer in control like blogs, iPods and Podcasts.

As these and many other events occurred, it was much like the ocean waters draining away from the shoreline signaling an impending tsunami.

Early in the new millennium came the dethroning of Dan Rather, Trent Lott, and the New York Times – all due to stupid comments or falsified news. All of them were exposed by the New Media. With those events, a series of tidal waves struck. The very foundations of the news industry and politics were shaken to their core.

But the difference with this New Media tsunami, is that the water hasn't receded. The New Media Revolution first felt in the arenas of politics and news is now sweeping through the entire culture. This Revolution is transforming everything in its path – including the customers and the marketplace you rely on for your success.

The Revolution Is Not New

In 1440, Johannes Gutenberg also ignited a Revolution. He did it by inventing a printing press – later called movable type. (So named, since it was a technology that allowed wood or metal letters to be moved on the printing plates.)

The main purpose of that technology was to mass reproduce Bibles, which up until that point were only printed in Latin. Since the majority of the public could only read their native language, while others could not read at all, the elite had to "reveal" the Scriptures to the public.

In just over half a century, the Revolution fueled by this one technology reached a flashpoint. Martin Luther nailed the 95 Theses on the door of the Castle Church in Wittenberg, Germany in 1517. These documents dispelled the power and efficacy of indulgences, and initiated a reformation of the power structure within the Catholic Church. With indulgences, bishops were playing God by selling forgiveness of sins.

The Revolution may have begun with Bibles, but very quickly, books of all kinds began to be translated, duplicated, and spread around the world at a rapid rate. This put information into the hands of common people instead of it being reserved for the elite.

Today, similar to Gutenberg's printing press, New Media is wrestling power and control of information from the elite once again.

New Media is turning mass media on its head. New Media is personal and participatory. It's about conversations rather than lectures. Information isn't being handed down from on high as if it's the Holy Scriptures anymore.

During the time of Gutenberg and Martin Luther you could say that the printers, publishers and writers were intellectual capitalists. They were using technology to transform the culture, and making a profit from that service.

Back then, the Elites were the popes, kings and lords who, as the elite, held the information and disseminated it to the masses as they saw fit.

Today, the intellectual capitalists are bloggers, talk radio hosts, and Podcasters. Intellectual capitalists are the innovative business people savvy enough to recognize the transformation empowered by New Media, who then adapt and flow with the changes rather than fighting them.

Now, the Elites range from the mass media to large corporations and the government. They are the monarchs of the modern day who are fighting tooth and nail to retain their base of power – the control and dissemination of information.

The Early Years Of The New Media Revolution

If we go with the viewpoint that the New Media Revolution began in the early 1990s, then talk radio must be seen as one of the earliest "tremors" to be felt.

Talk radio took a traditional mass media form – radio – and turned it into something participatory.

While we wouldn't consider talk radio to be part of the New Media that business people need to focus on for growth and profits, it is important to understand why it's so popular.

Why is it that a host like Rush Limbaugh has 25 million people a day listening to his radio show? It's because compared to a regular radio show it's participatory.

People want their voices to be heard. And they want to hear from other people who think like them. Whether they agree or disagree with the host, they want the opportunity to call up and speak their mind.

After the introduction of talk radio, the Internet entered the scene. As more and more people went online each year throughout the nineties, the New Media started to take shape. The proliferation of broadband access made it possible for waves of change to move very quickly.

Today, the Revolution has irreversible momentum. Yet, not everyone likes what's happening.

The Gatekeepers And Guardians Of The Status Quo

The New Media tsunami is thundering through the marketplace, transforming everything in its path. Now that you realize that the Revolution is about people, participation, and persuasion – it's time to share an even more important secret.

The secret is in the opportunity that entrepreneurs and small-business owners have; an unprecedented growth opportunity like never before in history.

WHY IS THERE SUCH OPPORTUNITY?

Because the institutions and power structures of the past are still unwilling to flex and flow with the transformation taking place.

The institutions that dominated the Industrial Era are having their power to control and influence the masses erode right before their very eyes!

Corporations, government, and mass media may seem like giants, but like the slumbering giant who groggily awoke and tried to chase Jack down the beanstalk, they also have many limitations. Not the least of which is speed.

As Jason Jennings and Lawrence Haughton stated in their book, *It's Not the Big That Eat the Small… It's the Fast That Eat the Slow*, the speed of innovation is the real competitive advantage in today's marketplace. Speed is not exactly what institutions and the mass media are known for.

Governmental Institutions

By institutions, we mean big universities, state or federal government and any other closed system. If you've been to your state's Division of Motor Vehicles, tried to get a local building permit, or dealt with the IRS, you know what we're talking about. You're dealing with a system that doesn't like to admit fallibility. A system where there's a long-standing hierarchy which seeks to protect itself.

Because of that, change (especially anything that appears to threaten existing hierarchies) is shunned as evil. Every possible effort is made to hide, minimize, or deride the truth of the transformational forces.

Corporations

Most corporations don't have a structure that allows for rapid adaptation. Many corporations today still operate based on the principles of the Industrial Revolution. They see employees as cogs in the machine, and consumers as a herd of unthinking animals ready to be sold black and white solutions.

Even Internet industries, which are supposed to be "cutting edge", reveal their thinking through their actions.

Take broadband Internet access for example. Broadband infrastructure was built for fast downloads – not for uploads. Even if you have cable or DSL, you can download quickly, but it takes much longer to upload files.

Thanks to the mindset shaped by the mass media, mass marketing, and mass distribution, these corporations didn't see people putting back in as much as they took out. They didn't think about people participating.

Newspapers And Network Television

This is another group fighting the New Media Revolution. Readership and viewership are dropping precipitously.

Every month there are stories in the mass media about how readership is declining. Newsrooms across the country have let go of a huge percentage of their workforce over the last decade.

Why?

Because people are tired of being told what to think with no option to participate and share their two cents worth.

The credibility and power of major newspapers are being eroded, and it's the New Media that's chipping away at that.

Sure there was the New York Times scandal with Jayson Blair, and a host of others that expose the fallibility of mass media in news reporting. But take a look at the more practical side of mass media related to business.

For example, in every town that Craigslist (www.craigslist.com) enters, the local newspapers (large and small) shudder in fear because they know their advertising and classifieds are going to plummet.

Craigslist is instantly searchable, always up-to-date, and interactive. For both advertisers and prospective buyers, dead tree papers are inconvenient, expensive, and completely non-participatory.

These guardians of the past may fight hard to protect the status quo, but in doing so, they're leaving a tremendous void in the marketplace – a void that fast-moving entrepreneurs and business owners will fill and profit from – if they take action sooner rather than later.

The Shakeout And The Current Opportunity For Fast Acting Movers

The shakeout between the fast and the slow has already begun. The slow will fail in their feeble attempts at preserving the old ways.

It reminds me of Neo in *The Matrix* at the end of part one, where Neo gets on the phone and says to those controlling and manipulating what people see:

> *"I know now what you're trying to do, and I'm going to let them all know."*

Now with the New Media, there is an army of Neos – hundreds of millions of change agents. They are passionate about participating in the marketplace conversation and transformation. And that strikes fear in the hearts of the entrenched institutions.

What Does This Mean To You And Your Business?

It means it's no longer "business as usual". It means you can't market, sell or manage the way you did even just three years ago.

It also means you can give yourself a tremendous competitive advantage when you understand the New Media Marketplace.

If you're in business and you're not already feeling these changes, you will soon enough. The New Media world of blogs, Podcasts, social networks, Wikis and more are enabling participation and connection like never before in history. If you want a head start on your competitors, it's something you must get involved with now.

It's not that you have to become a New Media expert. You don't even need to blog or Podcast every day. What it does mean is that you need to be aware of the New Media Marketplace and keep track of it even if you're not actively participating in it just yet.

Otherwise you can count on this - you will be pummeled by the whitewater of the tsunami when it hits you.

So, what makes the New Media Marketplace different? Is it really changing the way we do business from here on out?

You be the judge. Let's check out this brave new world… shall we?

"Toto, I've a feeling we're not in Kansas anymore.

We must be over the rainbow."

– Dorothy in The Wizard of Oz

The New Media Marketplace

chapter two

》The culture of the New Media Marketplace is very different than what we're accustomed to with traditional online and offline marketing. To succeed here, you'll need to make a few shifts in your thinking.

Your online mindset on marketing will have to be radically different from what's been done over the past decade.

The traditional style of advertising used by Madison Avenue and many Internet marketers is more about interruption than influence. Influence is what you need to turn strangers into friends and friends into customers.

What's going on in the New Media Marketplace is a digital reflection of what's going on in the real world. At the heart of this is an interactive, dynamic where insight and innovation are front and center. Creative ideas on how to develop new products, policies and services are what are driving the marketplace.

This new Marketplace can be summarized in one word, "caput." That is Latin for "head." From that word comes the word we know as capitalism. So, out of the head comes creation, information, education and wealth.

Capitalism is about private creation and ownership for the common good. It doesn't work unless what you're creating serves some kind of need or provides a solution. Thus, if you are not serving the greater good, you will fail. This is the opposite of a socialist system where everything is supported regardless of its validity.

Information, Education And Wealth

Anyone can create information. And if it's valuable information and it makes an impact, it becomes education. But only if it solves problems, removes pain, or increases pleasure does it bring wealth.

Not everyone who recognizes the New Media Revolution will make money in the marketplace. Some will contribute information, some will educate, but a precious few – the ones who truly understand how the New Media Marketplace works – will be able to generate wealth from it. Only those who can create, converse, and deliver value will do profit from the marketplace.

That's the main driver for you as an entrepreneur, business owner, sales professional or marketer entering into the New Media Marketplace. Create through participation, converse with your ideal audience, and deliver value.

Doing this successfully requires a shift in your mindset, but it can be done. If I can do it, anyone can. LOL! (That's laughing out loud in "Internet speak".)

It's No Longer Just The Information Age

We've heard since the advent of the Internet that information is doubling at an ever more rapid rate than ever before in history. Yet, it is clear that it's not just about the information anymore. We've now entered into the age of communication.

Information and education are still at the core, but the New Media Marketplace is about communication. It's about connection and participation. In a way, as we discussed earlier about the New Media Revolution, it's about stepping backwards in time. Human culture has always been centered around stories and personal relationships.

Going way back in history, starting before Christ extending through the 19th Century, the marketplace was based on relationships. Then we went through the Industrial Revolution, where expansion and economies of scale were the focus.

Now with technology, in a sense, we're stepping back while leaping forward. We're refocusing on personal connections while simultaneously expanding the reach of those one-on-one communications with incredible new technologies.

A client of ours is an expert on the barbarians active in Northwestern Europe after the fall of Rome. As we worked with him on his New Media Marketing Strategy, he's mentioned that if we could go back in time and grab a few of those guys and pull them forward in time and acclimate them to the New Media Marketplace, they would look around like we were insane for not all being incredibly wealthy.

Citizens of the Dark Ages could only communicate with a few people and it took them months to go and get new products. Now, we don't even need to see people face-to-face. We can communicate with them and connect with them at the blink of an eye.

That's a perfect example of what the New Media Marketplace is all about – communication and participation. Not about the one-way dictatorial diatribes of mass media or some cool new technology.

Unfortunately, after all the years of indoctrination by the mass media, that's a difficult shift in mindset to make for the average Joe.

But we're about to help you make this shift easier than anything. Throughout the chapters of this book, we'll be looking at how old school advertising differs from marketing in the New Media Marketplace. You'll also learn how to start taking action to get results with this new mindset.

Where The Wealth And Power Are

The age of communication requires exchanges, but creation of all those comments, conversations and bits of information builds a tremendous volume of data. Real wealth and power are not where you think. It's not necessarily reserved for the high-volume producers or high-traffic sites.

The greatest area of opportunity for many businesses lies in what's called the "Long Tail."

The Long Tail is a term coined by Chris Anderson in an article he wrote for *Wired* magazine in 2004. (Also the book of the same title, released in July 2006.)

It comes from a graphical representation that shows how the relatively few in any industry, market, or supply channel can appear to carry most of the momentum. They form what's called the "head."

All the smaller players or lower demand products trail off in a downward sloping curve. They form what is called the "Long Tail."

For a practical example of how this works, let's take a look at a graph representing the sale of music.

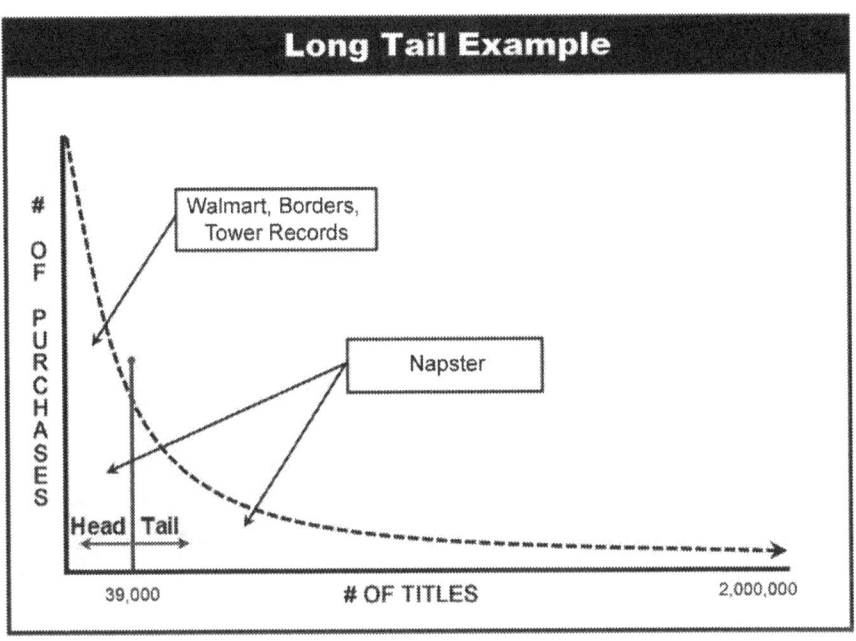

In the head, are the primarily off-line stores who look (at first glance) to be carrying the bulk of the volume in sales.

However, when you look closely, you'll notice that the number of titles available is limited only to the most popular artists, and only when purchasing an entire CD. When you move into the Long Tail, you see the sale of many more obscure song titles with an appearance of decreasing volume.

But the fact is that Napster has gained the loyalty of customers who either purchase or "rent" access (through a $15/month membership) to the same high demand titles in the head, along with nearly two million lower demand individual songs in the tail. The sum total of all the less popular titles in the Long Tail far outweighs the volume in the head.

By leveraging New Media delivery/consumption, and satisfying the desires of numerous musical micro-markets, Napster is able to compete with the big name stores via the Long Tail.

A competitor in the music field with an even tighter niche focus like Garageband.com (who focuses only on emerging artists) can do very well in an even lower volume Long Tail.

The music industry is just one example of how the marketplace is fragmenting into many sub markets. The same applies in nearly every other niche. The fact is that the old school ways of doing business and marketing will no longer work.

Your target audience is no longer huddled together waiting for you, your product or your message to appear.

When you learn how to capitalize on this trend of fragmented markets, you'll unlock the door to a treasure trove of marketing and business growth opportunities.

You may think that this is a philosophical way to look at a graph or a "cute" way to analyze it, but when you really look at it, you see how this is truly an insightful way to view the New Media Marketplace.

Amazon is a perfect example.

Amazon came on the scene and turned the book world on its head. Prior to Amazon, when you walked into a bookstore, there were a limited number of titles and a bunch of stodgy people who lauded their knowledge of books over you so that if you weren't an avid reader, you felt out of place.

Offline stores such as Borders and Barnes & Noble began to shift to deliver more of what the customer wanted in the off-line world, but Amazon turned the market on its head. Amazon operates in the "Long Tail."

An Amazon employee stated it perfectly when he said:

> *"We sold more books today, that didn't sell at all yesterday, than we sold today of all the books that did sell yesterday."*

You can go to Amazon and find any book you want. They even have sources for out-of-print books. A traditional bookstore could never serve those types of needs at the speed and convenience that online shoppers enjoy at Amazon.

Even today, traditional booksellers are woefully inept at delivering complete customer centric convenience.

This type of non-service frustrates me. Let's say it's Friday morning and I want to pick up 10 books for a project I'll be working on over the next week.

If I could walk into a bookstore and pick up the books I need, it would be easier, because I can just stop by the local bookstore and pick them all up. Instead, I'm frustrated every time I go to the physical bookstore, because they still do things the Old World way.

No matter whether I call ahead or just stop in, without fail, they'll only have five or six of the books I need. "Sorry" they tell me, "we'll have to order the rest in for you. We'll call you in a few weeks when the next shipment arrives" (grrrrrr) Can you relate?

Contrast that with Amazon, where even if it's Friday at midnight, I can have every book I want delivered directly to my doorstep all the way to Hawaii, the most remote island chain in the world, by Monday – all ten of them!

Even if they're out-of-print or obscure titles – there are no hassles, zero frustration, and I'm in complete control. I enjoy total convenience suited to my needs, even living on the most remote island chain in the world.

That's what the Long Tail is all about. And it's not necessarily just about what's happening online. The New Media Marketplace causes the online and offline world to mirror each other. (Almost like the supernatural world and the physical world. Ahhh, but that's a side bar

– I could go on and on about it, if you let me. Just rent the movie, *The Matrix*, and you'll see what I mean.)

Getting back to the huge amount of data in the Long Tail that must be navigated through. This ever-growing volume makes filtering the Long Tail an absolute necessity.

There's a quote by Paul Saffo from the *Institute for the Future* that makes it clear where the power of the New Media Marketplace is.

> *"You get large by allowing the many and the small to gather on your lawn."*

Think about that and let it sink in.

> *"You get large*
> *by allowing the many*
> *and the small*
> *to gather on your lawn."*

Makes more sense the second time you hear something that profound, right?

Isn't that what eBay has done? Yahoo!, eTrade, Wikipedia – all of these online and click-and-mortar crossovers – that's what they're doing. They are taking advantage of the Long Tail because that's where the true power lies.

This is a dramatically different marketplace that requires us to view it through a new set of eyes. The effectiveness of getting your message out to the masses using one or two mass media channels is decreasing daily.

The New Media Marketplace | 23

Successful marketing is about going to niche groups (or tribes,) creating a dialogue, and encouraging participation. (We'll share more on that in chapter three and chapter five.)

Is It World Wide Or World Live?

Another shift in the online marketplace is how we view the World Wide Web. The World Wide Web has been transformed over the last two years into the World **LIVE** Web.

Content is being created at such a rapid rate that Google, Yahoo!, and MSN have all completely revamped their search engine algorithms to reflect the LIVE nature of New Media.

If you try and do business the same old World Wide Web way, you're going to sink.

Why do you think we see all the top Internet marketers sharing all their "top secrets" they've been using for the last few years at big seminars around the United States? Do you think they're still using those techniques?

No, they're sharing what they've wrung dry and now that's going out to the masses of mid and lower level Internet marketers. And doing so will further accelerate the demise of those techniques.

The top Internet marketers are on to new ways to use New Media to create buzz and to build relationships. (They're just not sharing this with anyone else yet.)

Mobility Will Make It Happen Faster

You may have heard the term "third screen" by now.

Third screen implies that the television was the first screen, the computer was the second screen and now the third screen is seen on mobile devices like iPods and cell phones. The third screen makes the New Media Revolution mobile.

For many people over 35 years old, a third screen device is an amazing new convenience. For people under 25, it's a natural part of life. For most people in the latter age group, it's the television that's the third screen. The primary screen is the computer because of the Internet, and then the second screen is their mobile device.

While your target market may not be that age bracket, don't ignore what's happening. You need to be aware of these shifts because it's transforming the culture and the marketplace.

Just like rock n' roll changed the culture and came from the under 25 crowd in the late 1950's and early 1960's, the same thing is happening now with the New Media.

This is the demographic that most of the big marketers are going after.

They know that if they can influence kids while they're still under 25, they'll have them as customers for life. People are creatures of habit.

Marketers need a new way to effectively reach this demographic. As the New Media Revolution quickly spreads to other age groups, the same will soon be true in the entire marketplace.

»COACHES HINT: *Watch how the video game and music industries adapt their marketing to reach their target market. This is where you'll see where marketing is headed for all but the over-60 crowd.*

Participation Makes New Media

One seemingly unrelated example of the participatory nature of New Media is Google Video (video.google.com). It's a free service where you can upload your video content to the Internet. Google makes it searchable and you're able to store your high-bandwidth video content on Google's video service.

Why would they do that for free?

Why would they offer Gmail? Why would there be Google Notebook or Google Desktop?

Google is investing in this area because they realize they must move in a direction that reflects the participatory nature of the New Media Marketplace before competitors beat them to it.

They're allowing all of these uploads of video in order to monitor the activity of their consumers and then practice, modify, tweak and improve their indexing of that type of content to make completely searchable.

It's a great service, too, because as an entrepreneur or business owner you can offer that content for free or for a fee, and you, as the creator, keep up to 70 percent.

Another example is YouTube (www.youtube.com), which launched in early 2005 and already transfers more data each day than the Blockbuster movie chain does. It's incredible to see the amount of movement that's taking place in the New Media Marketplace.

YouTube went from zero visitors on a monthly basis during the Spring of 2005 to 12.5 million visitors per month in April of 2006!

That's because of the participatory nature of YouTube. It's not just video; it's an entire social networking community that allows commenting, connection, and interaction between people of similar interests.

Understanding these shifts and the underlying drivers of this is what's important. It's not about video. You don't even have to produce a video as a business owner if you don't want to.

We're just using these sites as examples to show you what the New Media customer wants. They want to participate and contribute. When they're able to do that, the numbers and the traffic go through the roof.

Look at MySpace (www.MySpace.com). Community membership and traffic expanded rapidly because of the demographics participating being primarily teens and young adults in their early 20s.

As we said in the beginning, teens don't see the iPod and the cell phone as a third screen, that's their second screen where their first screen is the computer. For those 40-45 and above, it's the third screen because the television is their first screen.

Online and third screen access may be gaining momentum more rapidly with the younger demographic, but how does it impact your target audience? How is it going to move the marketplace over the next few years? How is this going to change the marketplace overall?

You need to start thinking in that direction. You might not be able to make immediate changes, but as your mindset shifts, you'll be ahead of your competitors and ahead of the curve.

The key to succeeding in business in the New Media Marketplace is that you must flex and adapt. You need to flow like liquid.

As Bruce Lee would advise his students who wanted to become world champions in martial arts,

> *"Empty your mind, be formless. Shapeless, like water. If you put water into a cup, it becomes the cup. You put water into a bottle, and it becomes the bottle. You put it in a teapot, it becomes the teapot. Now, water can flow or it can crash. Be water."*

That's the mindset you need with the New Media Marketplace. This is where a huge advantage comes for the small business owner over the large corporations in that you are more flexible.

Your mindset needs to be flexible. Your content needs to influence both people and search engine spiders. This is different from the early adopters of New Media, who were passionate about the technology and the conversations, yet they were stuck at the information level.

It's not that all the old proven Internet and offline marketing principles go out the window. God forbid! They do, however, need to be molded, become liquid and conform to the New Media Marketplace.

Make sense?

We'll delve into more depth on how you can shift your mindset and capitalize on the New Media Marketplace in chapter five.

The Customer Is In Control

The New Media Marketplace is consumer controlled. We just mentioned how the top search engine algorithms are being adjusted based on live content that is being created by the second screen (by blogs, through social networks, and even multimedia content like Podcasts.)

It's all being more rapidly indexed by the search engines' spiders than could have been imagined even a year or two ago. The customer is driving that shift.

The consumer is driving all the research, conversations, and the success or failure of a product online.

Successful businesses that understand what's going on in the New Media Marketplace are eagerly involving customers in the configuration of their products. They're putting an increasing amount of control into the hands of their consumer.

Your customers will get what they want, whether they get it from you or someone else.

You will either learn what consumers and customers want in the New Media Marketplace, or you'll be trying to catch-up to your competitors who are already providing it.

The next step in your journey of successfully marketing in the new millennium is understanding the New Media consumer.

The New Media Consumer

chapter three

"There's a tiny door in that empty office. It's a portal, Maxine. It takes you inside John Malkovich. You see the world through John Malkovich's eyes, then, after about fifteen minutes, you're spit out into a ditch on the side of The New Jersey Turnpike."

– From the movie, Being John Malkovich

》 There are two different types of consumers in the New Media Marketplace:

1. Sassy & Savvy

The first type knows exactly what they're getting into with the New Media. They understand blogs and social networks. They know what Podcasting is and how to use all types of search engines to find what they want. They understand all of these individual components and even if they're not actively engaged in all of them, they "get it" when it comes to New Media.

2. Community Connectors

Then there are others who are being drawn into the marketplace by the convenience, interactivity, or the fulfillment of psychological needs. They're being drawn in by their ability to contribute and connect. This group doesn't necessarily understand what tools they are using, or how these New Media technologies relate to each other. They simply enjoy them for the convenience it brings them, and the connection they get through online communities.

A rapidly growing number of new people are entering this marketplace every single day from both groups.

The good thing is, regardless of whether they view this all as comfortably familiar or shockingly new, these New Media consumers have nine characteristics in common. And they have five simple needs that must be met if you're going to build a relationship with them.

First, the nine general characteristics:

Nine Characteristics Of The New Media Consumer

1. NEW MEDIA CONSUMERS WILL NOT TOLERATE INTERRUPTIONS

The cat is out of the bag and the word is spreading like wildfire. People have found out that they don't need to tolerate interruption marketing any longer. They're telling all their friends, who then tell all their friends, and so on, and so the secret is exposed.

Offline – TiVo® and other DVRs (Digital Video Recorders) are allowing people to watch TV shows and movies when they want. With a simple push of a button they can zap commercials out, turning a one-hour episode into an uninterrupted 40-minute show.

Online – Arbitron and Edison Media Research tell us that as of February 2006, 73% of home Internet users use a program to block email spam. 71% use software to block pop-up advertising and 50% block banner advertising. All these percentages are rapidly rising and are equally as high with Internet access at work.

On The Go – Nearly one in four Americans use an iPod or other MP3 player to listen to the news, get information, enjoy their favorite songs and create their own radio stations whenever they want, without interruption advertising. An equal number of people are watching video on the go with portable DVD players, but you can expect to watch this number go through the roof as the price on Apple's video iPods begin to drop.

Let's ignore for a moment all the inexpensive filtering and free blocking technologies that consumers have at their disposal.

Do you see something even more important going on here?

Consumers are clearly showing that they've had it with the interruptions of mass media and mass marketing.

The answer to successfully creating relationships with your ideal audience is not to find a way to circumvent their defenses. It's to get them to open the door and invite you in through influence, persuasion, and trust.

Fortunately, for the savvy small business owner, most corporations and marketers just don't get it. Their idea of adapting to reach their target market is shouting louder.

As we continue along in this book, you'll see how a New Media Marketing Strategy simply and elegantly delivers what both the consumer and you as the business professional want. You'll see how it's infinitely easier to build a mutually beneficial relationship rather than bash consumers over the head with something they hate.

2. New Media Consumers Are Eager To Share

When you build relationships with your target audience and customers, it leads to trust. When you have trust combined with personal loyalty that encourages them to talk about, share, and spread the word about you and your product, then you've got yourself a raving fan! The personal connection makes it so much easier to turn an ordinary customer into a lifelong, customer evangelist.

Beware:

If today's New Media consumer doesn't get their needs met, they will also share their disappointment with all their friends and family.

If they feel they have a relationship with you, it's very likely you'll hear it from them first.

If they don't feel like they have a relationship with you, or if they feel you're just some slick marketer trying to pull the wool over their eyes – watch out! Get ready for them to share their disappointment in multimedia format; leveraging the very same New Media tools to hurt you instead of help you.

Yipes!

Guess we should have mentioned earlier that the New Media comes with just as many warnings for the company who dares to ignore the New Media Marketplace, as it has advantages for the company who embraces it.

3. New Media Consumers Have Faith In A Free Market

This means they believe in people and the power of participation. They don't want to be told by some pointy-headed elite what's important and then not be able to interact, to express their own viewpoint. This is a principle you can glean from the mistakes of the news organizations born in the mass media era.

One of the reasons dead-tree papers (offline newspapers) are losing subscribers and continuing to let go of employees, is because that channel of mass media is based on a structure that puts some single-minded, disconnected elite on a pedestal. That person then doles out news and information as he sees the world, which often doesn't align with the pure facts – or resonate with the "common" person.

The problems we see with news organizations are similar to what we discussed in chapter one about bishops and the church elite during Guttenberg's era. They were selling papal indulgences to forgive people of sins, and structured things so that they were the only ones to control the Scriptures of the Bible. The information was handed down from "on high."

More and more people are becoming tired of the mass media's modern version of that approach because they are seeing a lot of what is being disseminated as "fact" as inaccurate, propaganda or biased. Sometimes the writer or reporter is at fault. Sometimes it's the news organization that they're involved with.

It could even be the advertisers for their paper or news channel that determines what news gets told, and what gets squashed.

Just recently we had an experience that shows how news organizations from the mass media era are guarding their turf in controlling the flow of information. In a recent article we submitted for one of our various offline weekly columns, we talked about how the free market power of business blogging is helping small business owners.

The article told the story of a small business owner who used his blog to bring to public light the missteps made by a company hired to do work for the Maine Department of Tourism. The company tried to sue him and tried to put him out of business, but he was able to fight back, get national attention, and ultimately get the case dropped – much of the thanks due to the power of New Media.

The editor told us we had to revise the content. We've been writing for this paper for over three years and in all that time, never had an article pulled. Now all of a sudden, this article was a problem.

The article was very instructive on the power of New Media and how small business owners can use it.

As is usually the case, the mass media doesn't take kindly to any opinion or idea different from their own. They're guarding their territory because it's a power base.

None of this goes unnoticed by consumers in today's marketplace. If you try to take information and manipulate it for your own benefit, your target audience and consumers will see right through it and run the other direction. In the meantime, they'll warn all their friends and family to stay far away from you or your company.

This is precisely why news and political bloggers rose so quickly and gained mainstream attention. People were flooding to their blogs to read their favorite author's take on the "news" and current events, in an uncensored manner that you won't see anywhere else.

No one is banning their article or their take on the news. And it's successful because it's the way people communicate naturally at the water cooler every day in America, or at parties with their friends.

Getting their news should be no different, and the multitudes are making that very clear with the swift rise of New Media channels all over the Internet.

4. NEW MEDIA CONSUMERS NOTICE INCONSISTENCIES

The World LIVE Web is so active and instant that inconsistencies and over-consistencies in what's being said or written in mass media outlets are brought to light in a matter of hours. More and more people realize there is an alternative source of information out there.

That source is the New Media Marketplace.

The New Media consumer base is growing because inconsistencies and "over-consistencies" are not being corrected by anyone in mainstream media.

Inconsistencies are pretty easy to recognize since there is a misalignment of "facts" while they're presented as reality.

Over-consistencies occur when you look at ABC, NBC, CBS, CNN, The New York Times, L.A. Times or the Washington Post and you see or read basically the same news from the same angle on each of those sources. The lack of variation just isn't natural.

People in general are not that agreeable. Just take office politics for a perfect example.

Inconsistencies and over-consistencies raise people's antennae and they're beginning to be aware of the manipulation that's been going on for decades.

With the World LIVE Web, New Media consumers can quickly find the source of facts that will either bolster or bust a story.

When you're using the New Media for business purposes, feel free to share your opinions from your heart. That will actually help people connect with you and allow you to build relationships more quickly with like-minded individuals. Just be sure that you don't manipulate the facts.

5. New Media Consumers Are Independent Thinkers

Independent thought is another major driver of the New Media Marketplace. You're an independent thinker. You proved it just by picking up this book. That's a requirement if you want to be successful as an entrepreneur, sales professional, marketer, or business owner.

Many people (some would say the vast majority of people) are not very independent in their thinking. They're more comfortable following.

But that doesn't mean they think of themselves as followers. Contradictory as it may sound, most people like to think of themselves as independent thinkers.

This feeling of independence and control is a critical, psychological need of people. If you can learn to fulfill this need for your customers, through your products and/or services, you'll have a tremendous advantage over your competitors.

6. New Media Consumers Are Loyal To People Not Brands

This is because connections are being made on a personal level with New Media. They will bypass others to buy from you because of loyalty.

That's a pretty powerful benefit, wouldn't you agree?

If they're treated properly, customers will not only buy your products, but they'll also spread the word by word-of-mouth marketing all across town, and all around the world using New Media methods of communication.

If they believe in you, what your product delivers, and the quality of your product, there's a much stronger linkage between you, your product and your customer. Infinitely more than there could ever be with a large corporation and/or a competitor relying on mass media marketing.

7. New Media Consumers Are Comfortable With The Long Tail

The term "Long Tail" that we discussed in chapter two may be more familiar to a seasoned user of New Media, but newcomers to today's online marketplace catch on very quickly to this concept.

These New Media consumers see there are tons of information sources out there. They usually don't care who gives them what they're looking for – just as long as their needs are met.

Since Google, Yahoo! and other blog specific search engines have shifted and made finding relevant information easier, the average person that does not understand anything about the New Media Marketplace can go online and be introduced to it immediately. They're comfortable with the Long Tail even if they don't know what it is.

Whew! That's good news for you! (Unless you give them this book, of course, and then they'll understand the concept just as you do.)

8. New Media Consumers Are Passionate

These are people who are often exploring their niche or an area of interest many hours each week. They're not just doing it for their job. They're involved, commenting, engaging and participating because they are passionate about something.

If that "something" is related to your product, service or business – that's great. If not, find an audience that is talking about things related to your company or has problems that you can solve.

9. New Media Consumers Are Very Conscious Of Character

Since the New Media Marketplace is based on relationships and the New Media consumer is loyal to people and not brands – that puts everything on a one-on-one, person-to-person level. Because of that, character becomes evident more quickly.

You can't hide behind your computer screen and use it as a mask.

People may have gotten away with that using mass media marketing, but with New Media it will become evident what your true character is in short order. So, if there's a character misalignment, you must take steps to re-align that right now.

A great book that helps align your character with your online presence is called *A Virtual Handshake* by Scott Allen and David Teton.

Go grab that today, and you'll understand how selling is taking place online more than ever before, creating virtual handshakes and different ways to meet eye-to-eye.

The Five Simple Needs Of The New Media Consumer

If you're going to succeed in connecting with customers today, you'll need to meet five needs that New Media consumers have.

These needs are not complex, and they don't require a huge investment in order to fulfill them, but they are necessary if you're going to stand out from the crowd.

The good news is that they're easiest to meet when you're harnessing the power of New Media in marketing your business.

NEED #1 – VALUABLE CONTENT

Remember earlier in chapter two when we looked at the three levels of contribution in the New Media Marketplace?

They were information, education and solutions (which leads to wealth.)

As a business owner you have to move your target audience from one to the next with increasingly deeper levels of valuable content.

At first, some people may be looking for information. Others may find you when looking for education (including research for buying decisions.)

In either case, you need to move those people up the ladder from one level to the next; then you both will get the end results you're looking for. They get their problem solved, which improves their life and you get the wealth, both financially and in the fulfillment of knowing that you satisfied someone else's needs, and helped make someone else's life better.

When you focus on the content that your target audience finds valuable, instead of just focusing on conversion, fulfilling this need will come much more naturally for you.

Need #2 – Consistency

New Media consumers want consistency in their sources in two different ways.

First – consistency in the delivery method of your content. This can be the posting frequency on your blog, how often you or your company publishes a Podcast, or how often you or someone from your company team interacts in targeted social networks online.

Second – consistency of character. What is your voice, your style? How does your character come across? Whatever it is, that should be consistent. Once somebody picks up *your voice*, you're that much closer to deepening the trust and loyalty with your customer.

Note: Using your "natural style" doesn't mean that if your communication skills are lacking, that you can continue in that, and use "it's just my style" as an excuse. You have to adjust and improve so that you can communicate and connect more effectively with all types of people from all walks of life.

NEED #3 – CONVERSATION, CONNECTION AND ENGAGEMENT

We've been talking about this principle all along, but this is a serious need that the New Media consumer has, and it must be fulfilled.

So how will you fulfill it?

The secret that most mass marketers don't understand is that the New Media consumer doesn't mind marketing. They're not averse to marketing. It's just that they want to be marketed with, not to.

That's key and is worth repeating. New Media consumers want to be **marketed with**, not to.

As you learn to harness New Media channels, this will become easier. And as you put these new strategies to work, you'll gain a huge advantage over your competitors.

NEED #4 – PART OF THE PROCESS

The customer is the programmer. They actually want to be part of the development of the product, service, or even the book that you're writing.

People want to contribute.

Meeting this need is a huge advantage for you. Think about it for a moment.

If a prospect or customer feels they've contributed to a product or service your company offers, do you think they are going to feel more or less motivated to buy and promote that product?

Of course, the answer is more! That's because part of them is in your product or service.

People remember being involved. So, when it's time to promote and get the buzz going to create interest that will help other people experience what they've experienced, they're going to get the word out – big time!

After all, their identity is on the line. If they helped contribute their two cents to your product, they'll be committed to making sure it's successful.

NEED #5 – RESPECT

This can be as simple as applying some or all of the *Ten Commandments of Marketing with the New Media* that we'll be covering in chapter fourteen. If you read and commit those to memory, they will encapsulate what respect means for the New Media consumer.

You're building relationships and rapport with good old-fashioned manners. On the practical side, you also have your natural and adapted communication style. Of course, you also need to respect their personal needs, wants and desires.

Reaching Out To The New Media Consumer

Now you have a good basic understanding of the New Media consumer. Combined with what you learned in chapter one and two, the New Media Marketplace is all making much more sense now.

You're probably wondering how you're going to cut through all the clutter and connect with this new breed of customer.

How will you initiate relationships, build trust, and deliver valuable content while still getting all *your needs* met as a business owner?

It starts by having the right tools!

Your New Media Toolbox

chapter four

"Riddle me this: when does a painter use a trigger instead of a brush? ... When he's a stickup artist!"

– *Riddler, From the Batman TV series*

》As a child growing up, my father taught me the value of choosing the right tool for the job. He showed me how the right tool could make even the most difficult job infinitely easier. It's a lesson I've used for profit in all my businesses since then.

At times I must admit it seems like I'm always saying "the right tool for the right job." There's a reason some phrases or proverbs are often used. It's because they accurately convey in a few words what would otherwise take a book to get across. The right tool for the right job is one of those phrases full of wisdom.

Imagine you've always dreamed of owning a historical home, and you've just bought an old Victorian home that you're having restored to its original glory.

As the contractors hammer away replacing the roof, you check the attic to make sure nothing of value can get damaged up there if anything goes wrong. As you're looking around in the attic, you discover an old map that's been dislodged from under one of the rafters as a result of all the banging.

To your surprise, it's a map that shows where the original owner buried diamonds in your backyard!

Now, you'd want to hurry and dig a hole to get the diamonds, right?

Picking up a shovel might seem like the *logical* thing to do. However, is a shovel always the *best* tool to use when you need to dig a hole?

If the soil is compacted and hard, a pick can make the job go a lot faster. If the soil is rocky, using a breaker-bar along with the pick and shovel is the best combination. That gets the job done a heck of a lot faster and with a lot less effort than a mere shovel.

What if things were not as you originally expected? What if the diamonds were, in fact, buried under what is now part of your concrete driveway?

All of a sudden, things get a little trickier. Even if you pay a team of twenty men to dig for the diamonds using shovels, picks, and breaker-bars – it could be months before you reach your goal.

It's a totally new environment now, and you need a totally new set of tools. Things you would have never thought of as necessary to dig a hole are now required. Self-powered tools like a jackhammer, a backhoe, and a dump truck to haul away all the debris are needed.

With these new tools, you and two helpers could reach the diamonds in a matter of hours.

Likewise, you have the same situation with the New Media Marketplace. The map to your future online marketing success has been laid out before you. You can see where you have to dig, but the tools you've been using are completely inadequate. You need some new equipment.

An artist can't paint with a gun, a thief can't scare anyone with a paintbrush, and today's business owner can't effectively market with the inadequate tools of the past.

With the first three chapters of this book underway, you now have a good foundation on how the New Media Marketplace operates and what New Media consumers want. So now, just like Tim Allen used to say on his TV show, *Home Improvement* …

"It's Tool Time!"

Your mastery of the New Media Marketplace will be much more manageable, more effective, and A LOT more fun when you have the right tools.

The New Media tools we're about to introduce you to are a lot like the super modified high-horsepower tools Tim used to demo on the TV show (much to his sidekick, Al's dismay.) Something would always go wrong. That's because in order for high-powered tools to do the work effectively, a well-thought out plan was required.

In the same way, you need to create a customized plan for your specific business and you need to employ the strategies in your plan properly if you want rich results. We'll help you get started on your plan in section two. But in this chapter, let's first roll out the tools you need and introduce you to the power each New Media tool wields.

In all, there are twelve New Media tools that business owners can utilize building buzz, branding, relationships, and sales. As you acclimate yourself to the New Media, you can customize a more advanced strategy to match more tools to your niche and goals.

For now, let's keep things simple with the six main tools that you'll need to be aware of as you begin marketing with New Media.

THE NEW MEDIA MARKETING TOOLS:

1. Business blogs
2. Podcasts
3. RSS
4. RSS Aggregators
5. Social Networks
6. Wikis

Some of these have already been mentioned in passing, but now we'll give you a more thorough introduction to each New Media tool you'll have working for you.

Later in section three and four of this book, we'll share some innovative ways that you can use some of the most powerful tools as secret weapons for your business growth.

Let's get started with the #1 most important New Media tool for your marketing success.

1. The Business Blog

Rather than launch into some boring (snore), technical definition of a blog, we're going to look at this New Media tool in a way that has more real-world relevance. A more contextual description that makes sense to you as a businessperson.

To understand the real power of the business blog, it's helpful to think in terms of **BLOG I³**. That stands for:

- BLOG Instant
- BLOG Interactive
- BLOG Intuitive

BLOG Instant

The first **"I"** is one of the most powerful aspects of the Blog, as it's the **instant** part of your blog or Podcast. You get instant publication, instant delivery of content, and near instant indexing by search engines.

A blog is best thought of in terms of software that allows you to publish new content to your site with the click of a single button.

If you can use Microsoft Word, you can use blogging software to start generating traffic, building relationships, and also achieve top search engine rankings very quickly.

Simultaneously, with that same click of the "publish" button on your blog, the software instantly distributes your content to subscribers, search engines, and specialized directories – letting them know you have new content for them to pay attention to.

This is HUGE! (Read that last paragraph again to let it sink in.) Powerful stuff, right!?!

In the past, when you put up a Web site or added a new page to an existing Web site, it just sat there waiting for people to come to it.

Now, thanks to the power tool, RSS (Real Simple Syndication, which we will cover in-depth in just a minute) your blog **automatically** updates blog-specific search engines, general search engines, your subscribers, and more, with one simple action.

Can you see why we're so excited about having you add this power tool to your New Media Marketing toolbox?

BLOG I*NTERACTIVE*

The second **"I"** is something your clients and prospects will love, because it's the **interactive** component of your blog.

It comes from numerous functions and applications of your business blog where your readers and prospects get to "touch" your product online, and reach out to you no matter where they live.

One interactive aspect is called **commenting**. This allows your readers or subscribers to post their own thoughts, comments, and questions quickly and easily.

Sometimes a person is simply agreeing with you or giving you kudos for some piece of great information you shared on your blog. Some comments can challenge an opinion or philosophy that you put forth.

Other times, their commentary is adding to the conversation. For instance, you may have posted a story you wrote about a news story related to your industry, and someone posts a comment, "Hey, great story! But the latest news is…"

Either way, as we've already seen, the ability for your clients to instantly interact with you is already built into the software.

There are several more interactive aspects to a blog. For example, **TrackBacks** are also an interactive component of a blog, but since that's a more technical topic, we'll set that aside for now and cover that in section two of this book.

Deal?

BLOG* I*NTUITIVE

The third "**I**" means a blog is easy for you to use. When your blog is structured properly, it's extremely easy for visitors to use and navigate.

Whether you have articles, audio, or video – or a combination of all three on your blog – it's all posted chronologically starting with the newest post, and working down to the bottom of the page.

The information you provide is easily searchable by virtue of the way blogs are put together.

Another aspect of a properly structured blog that makes it intuitive is that it's categorized. A blog can be categorized by both date and topic. That makes it extremely easy for anyone who is a first-time visitor to find content you've discussed relevant to what they're searching for.

In section two, we'll go into much more detail on how you can start putting together a blog that's effective for business marketing. For now, I'm sure you can see why we advocate using a well-structured blog as the center of your New Media Marketing system.

2. The Podcast

The simplest way to think of a Podcast is a multimedia file (audio or video) catching a piggyback ride on your blog posts for hassle-free automated delivery.

As you just read, with the click of one button on your new blog, your content is instantly syndicated to subscribers, customers, and search engines. Podcasting takes that single action and puts it on multimedia steroids by attaching a little tag (called an **enclosure**) that lets the recipient know they have an audio or video file waiting for them.

One of the most practical ways a business can use Podcasts is to create a regular, daily or weekly "radio show."

When people have subscribed to your show with easy-to-use software like **iTunes** (www.itunes.com), the multimedia file is automatically downloaded and added to their iPod or other MP3 player.

Then, when they grab their portable device and hit the road, the downloaded audio or video goes with them for mobile play. A copy also stays on their desktop to be played, replayed, or archived like any other computer file.

All this takes place seamlessly, without the subscriber having to do any extra work. They simply subscribe to your show, and the rest is handled automatically for them.

The result is complete convenience and complete control.

For you as a business owner, the best thing is that when you hit the "publish" button on your blog, a description of what your Podcast is all about goes out to blog-specific search engines and to Podcast-specific directories.

We like to think of this as free advertising for your business!

The Power Of Multi-Channel Leverage

One quick example of a way we create regular Podcasts without even creating new content is with the regular guest spot Deborah has on the popular "Wayne & Jane Radio Show" on the KBS Radio station.

Each week Deborah and Wayne discuss the big wins and blunders of the latest contenders from NBC's hit TV show, *The Apprentice*. The Wayne & Jane Show is one of Canada's most popular radio shows in the morning drive-time slot.

There are people who either can't listen in at that time, or they live somewhere else around the world.

We take the recordings from each Radio show interview and upload them to our business blog, which is set to automatically update our iTunes Podcast channel.

With that one simple action, thousands of other *Apprentice* fans around the world get to listen in to the commentary, coaching, and tips that Coach Deb shares with Wayne's listeners, and thereby get introduced to us as influence and persuasion experts.

Plus, unlike a LIVE Radio show that requires the listener to be listening to the broadcast at the very moment it's aired, our Podcast listeners can now participate in the conversation about *The Apprentice* candidates and add their comments through TheInfluenceCodeBlog.com.

As business owners, this is huge because we get worldwide recognition and exposure in a way that was next to impossible just a few years ago unless you had a syndicated Radio or TV show.

This is just one example of the power of Podcasting. We'll cover more innovative ideas on business uses for Podcasting in chapter 15 on *Podcasting for Profit*.

For now, the bottom line is that Podcasting is an extremely effective method for reaching new prospects with a New Media channel that quickly builds relationships and trust. It's quite amazing how simple and powerful the process is.

THE SKINNY ON HOW PODCASTING WORKS FOR BUSINESS

With a growing number of people flocking to Podcast directories for specific niche content every day, this creates huge opportunities for the fast-acting business owner who gets a jump on using this tool. (This is similar to the concept of the Long Tail we looked at in chapter two.)

Let's say you have a sales training company. You create a Podcast radio show about "sales successes and flops" on a weekly basis.

A business owner or sales manager goes to a Podcast directory such as iTunes or Podcast Alley (www.Podcastalley.com) and they do a search on sales or selling.

Up pops your Podcast radio show in the search results. They give it a listen, like it, and become a subscriber to your show. **Bam!** You're now connected with a new person who wants to hear what you have to say – every week.

Now you have an opportunity to be exposed to an entirely new group of people in a highly targeted audience who otherwise might not have ever heard of you or your services.

Once a subscriber has your Podcast loaded to their ipod, they can take it with them whether they commute to work, workout at the gym, or fly to a business meeting across the country. They can even listen to you on their car stereo with a cool little device that turns an MP3 player into their own custom radio station.

Even more important than the practical, on the persuasion and influence side – Podcasting instantly raises the relationship you'll have with your prospects and clients to a whole new level.

With an audio Podcast, you can now utilize voice intonation, character, and emotional connection all combined with complete convenience and great content for your listener.

Think about it. More and more people are looking to liberate themselves from commercial radio. They're looking to eliminate or minimize interruptions.

With Podcasting, you can quickly establish yourself as an expert and help people make their daily commute in their cars, or on the subway much more enjoyable with customized content that is automatically delivered for home, office, or mobile playback.

Oh yeah, and you become an instant radio show star!

3. RSS (Real Simple Syndication)

To keep this real simple (no pun intended ☺) an **RSS Feed** is an automated content delivery channel. When you hit the publish button on your blog, the content of your new post is automatically delivered to all your subscribers.

There's nothing extra you need to do. RSS is already integrated into your blog software.

So, if it's already part of blog software, why are we listing it as a separate New Media tool working hard for your business?

For one thing, it's because although RSS is a background tool and seems to be completely passive, there is an active component to it. Not the least of which is the fact that RSS bypasses email (and spam filters) and goes directly to the reader.

There's a lot more to RSS, but it can get a little "geeky," so we'll cover that in more detail in chapter 6.5.

RSS has nearly limitless basic and advanced business boosting applications. If you're new to RSS, the best thing to do is start using this tool from a consumer standpoint. The best way to do that is by utilizing the next tool on the list, an RSS aggregator.

4. *RSS Aggregators*

RSS aggregators dramatically reduce the time and effort needed to regularly check Web sites of interest for updates. The better aggregators create what could be considered your own "personal newspaper." Only it's a newspaper that's instantly updated and completely categorized to suit your personal tastes. It only includes what's important to you, and, of course – contains no interruption marketing.

The RSS aggregator does all the heavy lifting after you subscribe to an RSS feed. It checks for new content at intervals you determine, and it automatically retrieves the content you want, pulling it directly into your aggregator.

The RSS aggregator provides an efficient, consolidated view of all your subscriptions in a single browser display or desktop application. It makes digesting an incredibly large amount of information fast, easy, and even fun.

RSS aggregators are sometimes referred to as RSS readers, feed readers, feed aggregators or newsreaders.

Some Internet browsers like FireFox, (which is an open source browser you can download for free), or Safari, (which is Apple's browser for MACs), have RSS built right into the browser.

When you're using any of these browsers, you can actually read and manage your RSS feeds, as you surf the Internet, and add new RSS Feeds to your list with the click of a button.

Our favorite RSS aggregator for busy business professionals is called FeedDemon (www.feeddemon.com). This is a very powerful aggregator, which filters and helps organize content as it's pulled in.

FeedDemon also acts as a Podcast organizer, pulling in all your audio and video Podcasts and categorizing them in the same way as your other content. This little piece of software is a huge time saver!

On the outbound business side, just like RSS itself, you can be infinitely innovative with RSS aggregators.

For example, let's say you have premium content that you'd like to deliver to subscribers or customers. You can have custom-built RSS aggregator software designed for your specific needs. This custom application would allow you to share exclusive content with your clients by delivering it directly to their desktops.

It's basically like taking an RSS aggregator and branding it exclusively for you and your content. As with standard RSS delivery, an application like this avoids spam filters and email altogether.

As you can see, RSS and RSS aggregators can be very hard-working tools that act just like assistants on your New Media Marketing team.

5. Social Networking

Social networks are large groups of people that come together online. Within the larger group, people often form sub-clubs and groups that are even more niche-specific. *(Yes, my fellow entrepreneur, you're right on if you're thinking, "highly targeted audience." ☺)*

THERE ARE ALL KINDS OF SOCIAL NETWORKS

For example, some are gender specific – focused on women business owners or moms (like www.mommybuzz.com).

Some may be business focused, like ecademy (www.ecademy.com) or LinkedIn (www.linkedin.com). These are examples of social networking communities exclusively designed for the purpose of building business relationships.

Broader based social networking sites have gotten a lot of press lately with the astronomical growth rate of MySpace (www.myspace.com) and the data-rich newcomer TagWorld (www.tagworld.com).

These types of social networking sites are goldmines of cultural insight and indicators of coming trends.

As recently as the late 1990s, corporations would spend tens of thousands of dollars to get a fraction of the feedback and data you can now collect for free within specific social networks.

Social networks are not only great for interacting and engaging with your target audience. They also provide incredible opportunities for businesses to be able to observe, listen, and collect feedback from various demographics.

No matter how niche specific or general in nature some of the above examples are, they are all part of the New Media because they are participatory.

Social networks include discussions, forums, education, multimedia, and blogs. Everything going on in these communities is participatory.

6. *Wikis*

The sixth and final tool for now is the **Wiki**. Coincidentally, that name comes from a Hawaiian word that means *"quick."* A secondary meaning in Hawaiian is *"what I know is."*

To explain what the essence of a Wiki is, let's start with something that we've already reviewed – the blog. You can compare Wikis to blogs because they're both participatory.

A blog is the opinionated voice of one person or a small group of people posting new content on a consistent basis. People come and interact with that person (or group of people) using comments and TrackBacks.

With a Wiki, what people are participating in is **the creation of content**. The content or project is at the center with many people contributing to the development of the product, project or policy. It explicitly and very literally allows people to participate **on the same page.**

The Wiki has a number of big benefits that it brings internally to mid-sized and large companies. Wikis are transforming project management and eliminating a lot of back-and-forth email within companies. Wiki companies like Social Text, which makes a corporate or company specific Wiki software, are completely revolutionizing the way that companies manage projects online.

With a corporate Wiki, there's one project area and everybody knows where to go. Comments, contributions, additions, and updates – everything all happens on one page. It's all live, instantly updated, and infinitely editable.

Then we have Wikis for public use. A good example of a public Wiki is the largest Wiki site on the Internet called Wikipedia (www.wikipedia.org.) If you'd like to find detailed, technical definitions or historical background on any of the terms that we're mentioning in this book, or famous people you want to research, literally just about anything that you'd like to know – you can go to Wikipedia and find it.

In the case of Wikipedia, here's how it works.

Someone creates a new definition, description, or brief biography. That initial content can be added to, expanded on, or clarified by other people who decide to participate on Wikipedia.

Teams of monitors keep an eye on things to make sure that nothing is being done that is destructive.

To show you the power of participation, Wikipedia.org now has more than 12-times the edited content than is in the entire Encyclopedia Britannica. Wikipedia is huge and growing rapidly with each passing day.

It's only five years old, and already has over a million pages in English alone. It boasts more daily visitors than CNN or *The New York Times*, and it's open-source (which means it's free.)

Nobody's paying for it, and there's no advertising (yet.) That's what the New Media is all about – participation and convenience.

It's Not The Tools Nor The Technology That Are Your Keys To Success...

As you read about these New Media tools, remember that no matter how hard they work for you and your business, it's not the technology that's most important – it's your mindset.

New Media Marketing is about people, participation, and persuasion. As we said earlier, once you grasp and understand the culture of the New Media Marketplace, you'll gain the first mover's advantage over your competitors. An advantage that gives you not only positioning, but experience, too. That experience is what makes it more difficult for latecomers to catch up.

You don't have to understand every intricacy of the technology to benefit from it. Leave that to the geeks and programmers. You can pay people to do that stuff.

As a leader and innovator, what you need to focus your time on is the same place where you'll get the greatest return for your investment – developing your own New Media Marketing Strategy™.

> **GRAB YOUR $297.00 GIFT — FOR FREE!** «

For more money making ideas on using business blogs and other New Media tools to market and grow your business -- remember to grab your $297.00 Coaching Bonus for FREE!!!

Go to FreeNewMediaCoaching.com
(Hurry! While supplies last.)

The New Media Marketing Mindset

chapter five

*"Be like water making its way through cracks.
Do not be assertive, but adjust to the object, and you shall
find a way around or through it. If nothing within you stays
rigid, outward things will disclose themselves.*

*One should not respond to circumstance with artificial
prearrangement. Your action should be like the immediacy of
a shadow adapting to its moving object. Your task is simply
to complete the other half of the oneness spontaneously.
In combat, spontaneity rules; rote performance
of technique perishes."*

– Bruce Lee

》 All that we've discussed so far presents incredible entrepreneurial opportunities. The New Media Marketplace presents huge opportunities for established businesses as well. And as we discussed earlier, the decided advantage goes to the small business owner.

Back in chapter two we mentioned how Bruce Lee explained adaptation to his martial arts students by using the metaphor of "being like water." What he meant was that when you pour water into a container, the water becomes the shape of the container it's poured into. It flexes, flows, and adapts.

The vast majority of large corporations aren't nimble enough to adapt. They can't be like water. They can't form themselves to a new glass, because they've gotten so used to the shape they've created for themselves.

When you take corporations or any business owner poisoned by the mass media mindset and metaphorically pour them into a glass of a new shape – they break the glass.

Have you ever poured ice-cold water into a glass heated by the sun on a hot summer's day? I just did that yesterday, and one of my favorite cobalt blue glasses cracked!

As Bruce Lee shared in his metaphor, water can flow or it can crash. Those who hold onto the mass marketing mindset will crash.

The entrepreneur, innovative small business owner, or sales professional has a greater natural ability to flex, flow, and adapt quickly. But just because you can, doesn't mean you will.

We are all at one level or another an unconscious product of our past. You may now consciously understand and agree that the New Media Marketplace is about people, participation, and persuasion. However, the bonds of your past must be completely severed in order to capitalize on the opportunities that surround you.

The Industrial Era was about size and economies of scale. Glenn Reynolds in his book, *An Army of Davids,* does an excellent job of detailing how the power has shifted from the mega-corporations to the little guy in everything from marketing to astronomy.

In this chapter, what we're concerned with is not what's going on externally, it's about what's going on inside you head. It's about creating a shift in your mindset.

Breaking Out Of The Sheep Pen

The Industrial Era was all about training sheep. I wrote a paper in my junior year of college for a sociology class where I covered this in detail. I still remember that paper whenever we have the opportunity to sit and "people-watch" as we travel around the country.

The paper was all about how people raised in the mindset of the Industrial Revolution act a lot like sheep.

Sheep are rather patterned creatures. They're not too independent in their thinking. Although they might occasionally think the grass is greener on the other side, they rarely break out of their fenced area.

Instead, they stretch their heads through the barbed wire eating what they can reach on the other side. Then, they go right back to their safe little life inside the pen with the rest of the herd.

Chapter Five

My college term paper covered life from grammar school through adulthood, and I included my theories on how college is the training ground for corporate sheep pens. Even though I backed it all up with research, I was taking a big risk with my topic since the paper was to account for 2/3 of my grade for that semester.

Luckily, I had a professor who either took pity on me, or understood where I was coming from as a 21-year old business owner, because I ended up with high marks. ☺

Seriously though, stop and think for a moment how the entire U.S. educational system is set up. It's an antiquated system that's still based on the Industrial Era.

You're in grammar school. The bells rings, you move from class to class, and you're told what to do.

Go to high school and it's not much different.

Get accepted into college and you get indoctrinated by (most) professors who want you to follow directions and conform to (their) norms.

Even when they incite so-called "independent thought," it's really not independent at all. Students are really being manipulated to believe that they're thinking independently, but they're really just being pressured to follow along with the rest of the herd.

Fraternities are no different. It's not called "hazing" for nothing.

The truly innovative or independent thinkers are the ones who are "kept in line" with the threat of poor grades or shunned as fringe whackos like John Nash during the years he developed his Game Theory (which later won him a Nobel Prize.)

Unless you attended a private, Montessori, or charter school, chances are you experienced an educational system designed to prepare you to work in a corporation (the modern factory.)

From grammar school to high school to college, it's all designed around and based on, the Industrial Era model.

A system where people are happy being "good sheep." People blissfully "bâââ" their way through life. Kids are treated like sheep and therefore, in many ways begin to think like sheep.

Their brain never gets a chance to utilize its powerful, creative abilities.

Understandably, it takes effort to break free from all that bondage. You're reading this book, so we already know that you're an independent thinker, and you enjoy expanding your mind with innovative thoughts and ideas.

Even if you have climbed to a leadership position in your company or struck out on your own to run your own business – there are still voices from the past whispering in the dark corners of your head. Whispers that impact your business decisions.

The shouts of Madison Avenue and mass media only serve to further suppress innovative marketing ideas by making you think mass marketing is the answer.

The mass marketing mindset has permeated business thinking from the smallest mom-and-pop operation to the largest corporations in the world.

Before we begin to look at the more practical actions you can take to get started marketing with New Media, we have to spend some time helping you create a new mindset that will allow you to flex and adapt so you can flow like water.

Profiting From Independent Thought

In the New Media Marketplace, we've touched on the fact that people are so active because they want independence. The human spirit inherently wants freedom.

It's why no other country has ever done what the United States has done. We put freedom at the core of our government; freedom at the core of our existence.

Deep down in the soul of every person, no matter where they live, there is that yearning for freedom, for independence.

When the marketplace begins to shift in the direction where independent thought and freedom are nurtured, you see the explosion of interest and the explosion of interaction online. That is going on right now, as you turn the pages in this book.

It's in response to what people have been yearning for deep down inside; it's in response to something that's been suppressed for the last 100-years of Industrial Era thinking and mass media domination.

If you're in business and you're not already feeling these changes, you will. The New Media world of blogs, Podcasts, social networks, Wikis and other New Media tools is something you should be involved with so you can get a head start on your competitors.

It doesn't mean that you have to become some sort of New Media expert. It doesn't necessarily mean that you need to jump in today and start blogging or Podcasting yourself every day.

What it does mean is that you need to be aware of what's going on in the New Media Marketplace and keep track of it, even if you're not actively participating in it yet. Otherwise, you'll never be in a position to profit from it, as the future quickly becomes your present.

This Is Where Lateral Thinking Comes In Handy

Lateral thinking is an innovation process where you take proven processes, principles, or trends from a seemingly unrelated industry, demographic or topic and figure out how you can apply them in your business.

No one else in your industry may be doing anything like what you'll come up with. Many of your peers may even think you've gone off the deep end. But this is one of the simplest and most effective ways of innovating and gaining a huge competitive advantage.

Just think of Amazon, eTrade, or eBay. Each took principles proven in other industries and applied them to the one they were entering. As a result, they shook their competitor's foundations to their core. They each knocked well established and entrenched competitors for a loop.

And they each did it by applying lateral thinking.

It's the same thing here. As you begin adjusting your mindset to market with the New Media, you'll begin noticing things that at first glance seem unrelated to your business. Like for instance, how teens prefer to get their information.

Instead of thinking to yourself, "that's not my target audience," you need to look beyond the obvious using lateral thinking. When you do, you'll discover new approaches that will give you distinct advantages that are near impossible to be copied by your competitors until it's too late.

To carry the teen demographic example further, what could you learn from observing how teens are communicating? Besides the obvious fact that these same teens will quickly become twenty-somethings and thirty-somethings, there is a more immediate impact for your business hidden in their activities.

Much of the New Media is already so integrated into their lives, that they're not even cognizant of the level of efficiency they're experiencing. As they go about their daily lives, the adults who come in contact with them are noticing the immediate efficiency that can be gained by adapting some of the New Media practices children today take for granted.

That's why we see New Media being integrated into mainstream life much faster than computers, Internet, or broadband access ever did. That obvious efficiency and ease of use is what's causing New Media to spread across multiple generations more rapidly than any other cultural shift in the past has ever been able to.

The good news is that when you practice lateral thinking, you'll find your New Media mindset will develop rather quickly, and you'll find amazingly simple solutions right in front of your eyes.

A Practical Example Of Lateral Thinking Using Third Screen Marketing

Let's say you're planning an ongoing promotion for your customers and prospect list to let them know about dinner specials at the restaurant you own.

Before you spend the time, money, and effort to have hundreds of postcards printed and mailed – stop!

Think about a New Media activity that you could use instead.

You could completely shift your mindset by asking a different question. A question like, "What's something I see my kids doing every day that I could use to reach my clients?"

The very act of asking questions causes your mind to create new connections between the neurons traveling across the frontiers of your brain. It creates new neural pathways.

As you're making new connections and pathways in your brain, you're shifting your mindset and creating new possibilities – new opportunities that "patterned thinking" will never reveal.

Before you know it – **BAM!**

It hits you like a series of smiley faces on your cell phone screen! Why not **use text messaging** to instantly get the word out to your clients?!

With just a little lateral thinking, you just reduced your advertising costs to nearly zero, made the process instant, and with some planning, you could make the regular updates relevant and fun (yes that's right – fun!) for people on your list who have given you permission to contact them.

Even Donald Trump is adapting his mindset to integrate and profit from the third screen.

If you look at his age and the brick-and-mortar business that he's in, you may question why he should care about New Media.

Trump knows that New Media is driving the culture. If you watched the spring 2006 Apprentice TV show series, you noticed that throughout the show he introduced the marketing power of text messaging.

People are making money off of the third screen using simple text. They're using it to create profit-producing buzz for their businesses.

Keep in mind that even something as simple as marketing with the third screen must be done differently than mass media and traditional advertising firms would approach it.

If it's to be successful, it cannot consist of old-school interruption advertising. Otherwise, people will just automatically tune your message out. It must be done with connection and persuasion in mind. It should be buzz-worthy, clever, funny, or entertaining along with being relevant to the person receiving the message.

That's just one example of how you can start using your lateral mind. Look at common promotional activities in your business, or what other innovative businesses are doing. Then ask yourself how you can use New Media to make it work in your business or profession.

By thinking laterally, you can innovate more quickly to create buzz about your business, product, service, restaurant, etc. with third screening or any New Media Marketing channel that's appropriate.

Web Marketing 1.0 vs. Web Marketing 2.0

Another way to help you facilitate a faster shift to a New Media Marketing mindset is by using a comparison to the past. To set this up, let's take a look at Web Marketing over the last decade compared to Web Marketing that will work in the new marketplace.

The initial decade of Web Marketing was essentially traditional mass marketing applied to the Internet. It started innocently enough with mass email campaigns and classified ads. These were obvious and direct transfers from the offline techniques used by direct marketers and local advertisers.

Then you had banners, pop-up ads, and all forms of interruption marketing proliferating as the competition increased.

As traffic increased, and the amount of data being indexed by search engines began exponentially increasing, we saw the mass marketing mindset kick into overdrive. Tactics to interrupt and grab our attention got more obnoxious, and more aggressive.

So, as we compare this to marketing that will work better in today's online marketplace, we've listed twelve general components that should be considered as you develop an effective marketing strategy.

We've labeled the first decade of Internet Marketing as Web Marketing 1.0. And we've labeled New Media Marketing as Web Marketing 2.0.

The New Media Marketing Mindset

Web Marketing 1.0 vs. Web Marketing 2.0		
Concept:	**Web Marketing 1.0**	**Web Marketing 2.0**
Primary Focus:	"Eyeballs"	The Whole Person
Communication Avenue:	One-Way & Passive	Two-Way & Interactive
Generating Action:	Limit Choices, Coerce, & Trigger	Educate & Win Trust
Immediate Goal:	Conversion to Sale	Stranger to Friend
View of Customers:	Herds (unthinking followers)	Tribes (cellular & social)
Perceived Control:	Company	Customer
Lifetime of Effectiveness:	Moment of Decision	As Life Happens
Positioning:	Interruption	Influence
Delivery and Consumption:	Single Channel	Multi-channel, Multimedia, & Mobile
Conversion Style:	Dictatorial	Consultative
Development of Trust:	An Event	A Relationship
Word of Mouth:	Synthetic	Organic

Remember, the new version is an upgrade, not a replacement.

When we speak at seminars or marketing workshops around the country, someone will always ask if we're advocating the elimination of all the Internet marketing strategies of the past.

Our answer is an emphatic – NO!

Sure, there will be certain strategies and tactics from Web Marketing 1.0 that you will no longer use. You can essentially count on eliminating anything that's based on interruption. But there are many proven direct response and Internet marketing strategies from Web Marketing 1.0 that can and should be carried through to Web Marketing 2.0.

Think of the comparison being just like upgrading any software program you have. Version 1.0 may have had bugs that caused errors, it may have used excess computer resources, or maybe version 1.0 will no longer run on the operating system of the new computer you just bought. The program is in serious need of an upgrade if you want to continue using it.

- The bugs in this analogy, are the tactics of interruption.
- The excess resources are all the extra hours and dollars you must spend trying to outsmart the marketplace and cheat the next search algorithm shakeup at Google and Yahoo!.
- The operating system relates to the fact that it's no longer the World Wide Web; it's now the World LIVE Web.

Moving to Web Marketing 2.0 is not an excuse to ignore the principles of good sales copy. It's not an excuse for ignoring the strategies of good direct response marketing. All the aspects of good marketing continue; however, the way they're presented to the marketplace and the timing of their introduction into the relationship will to be very different than ever before.

Most businesses (both large and small) are continuing to market online with the mass media mindset.

This is good news – for YOU!

Some won't make the shift to the New Media Marketplace because they think that they're making money on $4 per click Google AdWords. Many more will not make the shift because they don't understand human psychology, and they fear the customer having more control.

Study the comparison table we provided and let the contrasts marinate in your brain. As an innovator and independent thinker, you'll soon find yourself naturally shifting to the New Media Marketing mindset.

Now that you're all primed and ready to start getting results, let's show you how to start building what will become the core of your New Media Marketing Strategy.

Section II

≫Business Blogging Secrets Revealed!

Blogging For Your Business Is Not What You Think

chapter six

"When the man with a pistol meets the man with a Winchester, the man with a pistol is a dead man."

– Ramon Rojo in Fistful of Dollars

>> In chapter four we discussed the basic description of a business blog. In this chapter you'll learn what blogging for your business really means when it comes to getting results. You'll see why the business blog must be the center of your New Media Marketing Strategy.

So… why are blogs gaining mainstream popularity so quickly? What's the attraction? Why is it so darn powerful when applied to business?

The answer is quite simple when you consider the history of marketing and communication. A blog exponentially multiplies the world's oldest, most favorite and trusted form of information sharing – word of mouth. People love sharing what they know with like-minded friends.

Think about it. Who do you trust the most to give you advice, recommendations, and information about opportunities, purchases, or choices?

If you're like the vast majority of people, it's the opinion of someone you know and trust – someone who you feel is just like you.

That type of trust comes from personal communication, conversations, and relationships built with people who share a common interest. When your blog is integrated into a complete New Media Marketing Strategy, it delivers all that and more.

Blogs provide the public with a more reliable way of getting news and information free from mass media manipulation and interruption marketing.

Blogs have moved from being a tool for publishing digital journals and commentary. Now, hundreds of millions of people are using blogs, some without even realizing it.

What this means for business owners and savvy politicians is that your markets are organizing themselves into tribes engaged in digital conversations.

Consumers are more in control than ever before and they are controlling the conversations on the Internet. Blatant advertising and marketing messages are being shunned.

Consumers want a more personal business experience where they can ask questions, offer feedback and have more facts before purchasing (or voting). Consumers and voters alike want control, and now, thanks to blogs and other New Media tools they have it.

Blogs allow you to build relationships around your brand, your business, your products and services. Relationships are the key. The rules of engagement have changed. Your markets are faster, smarter, and more organized. Now, business blogging positions you where no Web Marketing 1.0 method has ever gone before.

Blogs are search engine magnets whose viral link sharing capabilities allow ideas and traffic to be shared quickly and broadly. To get the benefits we've shared here, you must be business blogging as opposed to following the example of personal bloggers or your average political blogger.

> **»BUSINESS BLOGGING SECRETS REVEALED«**
>
> *Every blog post is viewed as a separate Web page by the search engine spiders.*
>
> *This is great news if you're looking to optimize your own Web site by using your blog as part of your main*

Business blogging opens the door to the world of exponential leverage for the average small business owner. Now, whether you live in Honolulu, Hawaii; Boise, Idaho; or Sydney, Australia; you can use blogging as a business multiplication tool that puts word-of-mouth marketing to work for you.

A few of the practical ways you can use a business blog:

- **Increase targeted traffic to your site**
- **Reliably boost your search engine rankings**

- ❑ **Build rapport and trust for more sales**
- ❑ **Multiply the lifetime value of your existing clients**
- ❑ **Prove your expertise as a respected authority in your niche**
- ❑ **Transform your clients into raving fans and customer evangelists**
- ❑ **Replace or complement your email newsletter for 100% delivery**
- ❑ **Generate press exposure and offline media coverage**

Blogs are not just used for sales, marketing and buzz. There are dozens of business areas where blogs can help improve information flow and improve efficiency.

Here are just seven ways that a business blog can boost performance internally in your business:

1. Project development and management for enhanced collaboration among team members across the hall or across the world.

2. Centralizing company information and distribution that eliminates duplication and redundant research.

3. A nearly instantaneous client and customer feedback engine that allows companies (large and small) to nip consumer issues and complaints in the bud.

4. Reducing email overhead and improving general team management by answering a question once, and only once.

5. A low-cost, instantaneous update system that automatically distributes premium "must have" information to clients and customers – with no worries about delivery issues or spam filters.

6. Organization and coordination of your in-house and outsource agent teams.

7. An online, creative think tank where internal company teams or industry peers from across the country can mastermind on a topical basis.

There are actually dozens more! In fact, the number of business boosting blogging applications is only limited by one's imagination.

To help stir your thinking even further, you can **download the free whitepaper** "*21 Creative Way To Boost Business With Blogs*" from the resource area at AdvancedBusinessBlogging.com.

> **》》 BUSINESS BLOGGING SECRETS REVEALED 《《**
>
> *Blogs are powerful drivers of Internet traffic because they deliver content that is fresh, timely and, frequently updated around focused topics and themes. All of these characteristics make blogs top power tools for search engine ranking and online marketing.*

> **》》 BUSINESS BLOGGING SECRETS REVEALED 《《**
>
> *When it comes to online marketing, quality content attracts both human visitors and Internet spiders alike. Organic search results are one of your main traffic drivers. The number one priority for marketing a product and service with a blog is to get your site content into the search engines for keywords. This will deliver targeted customers and prospects straight to your door.*

Personal Blogging Vs. Business Blogging

Personal blogging is done by all types of individuals young and old. They tend to publish articles that voice their opinions on a wide and scattered range of topics. Personal bloggers typically find it fun to document their personal lives, rant, or talk through stream-of-consciousness tangents.

Business blogging is done by business owners or paid employees within a company. These blogs have a narrow focus on the interests that are important to the target audience of the company, and have a common theme even when written by multiple individuals. Business blogs are used to promote products or services that help drive revenue and profits. They're used to increase reputation, credibility and authority with customers, vendors, and partners by publishing content that demonstrates knowledge and expertise within a given industry, market segment, or niche.

What Is The Difference Between A Blog And A Web site?

There are some important differences between a blog and a typical, static Web site. Here's a quick summary of how blogs are different from a regular Web site.

Blogs Are Different In The Following Key Ways:

- You don't need a Webmaster for regular updates.
- You can publish directly from your computer. (If you can use Microsoft Word, you can maintain a blog.)
- You can easily make changes to content with instant updates and minimal effort.

- There is no need for complex uploading of files to the Internet.
- There's no HTML or any other type of program code for you to learn.
- Your site content is automatically archived both chronologically and by the categories you create with just the click of a button.
- You interact with visitors through the built-in commenting feature.
- You get instant syndication of all your content; so one post (audio, video, or written word) goes out to thousands of subscribers and traffic sources with the push of one button. (This is done using RSS which we'll cover in detail in Chapter 6.5)

> **» BUSINESS BLOGGING SECRETS REVEALED «**
>
> ☒ **Blogs are NOT mere online journals.** *(At least not for the savvy business owner or marketer.)*
>
> ☑ *Blogs ARE instant publishing tools that allow you to easily update your content, create relationships, and build trust with your target audience.*
>
> ☒ **The power of blogs is NOT in the technology.**
>
> ☑ *As cool and convenient as blogs are for business marketers, the power of blogging is in the two-way conversations that create personal connections.*

☑ *Blogs become a personal extension of the author who builds relationships by responding to the feedback from clients and readers.*

☒ **Blogs are NOT a billboard just for press releases, product updates or company news.** (*Snore... zzzzzzzzz*)

☑ *Blogs ARE an open door to communication where customers and prospects can voice their opinions, contribute to product development, and become part of your company family.*

☒ **Blogs are NOT to be ignored as a passing fad.**

☑ *Blogs ARE so popular and have grown to wield so much power so quickly that innovative marketers are now using them as accelerators for everything from search engine optimization (SEO) to hubs for a complete New Media Marketing Strategy.*

When mega-Internet players like Google and Yahoo! alter their entire business models to adapt to a "trend" – you can bet it's not a passing fad.

Pulling Back The Curtain To Meet The Wizard Of Blogs

chapter 6.5

"The beneficent Oz has every intention of granting your requests!... But first, you must prove yourselves worthy by performing a very small task. Bring me the broomstick of the Witch of the West."

– The Wizard, from the movie *The Wizard of Oz*

》To appreciate the power of the automated technology you have at your disposal with blogs and Podcasts, let's pull back the curtain and expose the wizard at work on your business blog.

Using the movie, *The Wizard of Oz* as a metaphor, let's divide the blog into two sections.

First – what's in front of the curtain. The things the public sees. Like the things you'd see along the yellow brick road.

Second – we'll take a peek behind the wizard's curtain to show you what your business blog does for you automatically.

The Yellow Brick Road

This is the public roadway, where you and your audience walk freely. It's where your content is on display for all to see.

A business blog has a number of important components that work hard for you and your business. One of the central features of a blog is what's called the Blog Post.

A Blog Post is composed of:

- **The Main Body.** This is where your main content resides. It can be an article, pictures, a Podcast with a summary of the contents, or a video. This is the content that you're using to connect with people in your target audience.

- **The Date/Time Stamp.** The date and time stamp is for the recording of the day and time of your entry. It's also what your chronological archives are based on.

- **The Post Title.** The Blog Title gives a description of what each post is all about.

Another way you can think of a blog post is as an individual article or Web page. Your posts (or articles) are published in chronological order with the most recent article listed first or most prominently on the home page of your blog.

Your post is the centerpiece of content for your business blog, but there are optional components that are available with many blogging software packages. These can be enabled through a simple administration panel on your blog.

They include advanced calendars, custom archiving, the addition of reference links, filtering options, and a host of tools for advanced search engine optimization.

Five more public components to optimize on your business blog:

1. Blog title and description
2. Post titles
3. Categories
4. Archives
5. Comments

Your **Blog title and description** must appeal to your niche and contain targeted keywords for relevancy in the search engines. Build up curiosity in the minds of your visitors in each title, so they won't be able to resist clicking on your post.

Post titles must contain keywords – if you want to maximize your search engine optimization. When your keywords won't fit naturally in a post title, be as creative as possible.

Categories are always titled according to the keywords you are targeting. This really adds a high level of relevancy to your blog. Plus, it creates natural divisions of your content for visitors to your site. This allows people to use portions of your blog that are important to them without wasting time.

> **BUSINESS BLOGGING SECRETS REVEALED**
>
> *Set up your categories to strategically match up with your top 20 keywords, and you'll quickly see results as your keywords are optimized in your search engine rankings.*
>
> *Remember – you can always add categories as you go along. Don't sweat it. Just get started.*

Archives serve as a historical reference to previous articles. What's fantastic about the archives in your blog is that each post is positioned as a single topical page to the search engines. Plus, archives allow you to create an in-depth article history rich in keywords bringing you targeted traffic over and over again for years to come.

Comments should always be allowed, and encouraged. This promotes personal conversations and connection. You are saying to your audience that you are accessible and approachable.

HINT: Use compelling or controversial questions to engage your readers.

> **BUSINESS BLOGGING SECRETS REVEALED**
>
> *When you comment on another person's blog, add a link when you sign your comment and include the keyword or phrase you want to rank in the search engines. Do this on a blog with a good page rank and good traffic, and Google will find you quickly while you get targeted, referral traffic.*

Behind The Curtain

Technically, a blog is a simplified Content Management System (CMS). What's great about a Content Management System is that it allows you to easily publish to a Web site and manage content without having to know how to program code or hire a Web-content administrator. Once it's set up, your business blog will have an easy to use administration area that allows you to intuitively manage all your content.

There are a number of automated actions that work on your behalf with this system. And with these functions, the blog wizard is hard at work behind the curtain turning your business blog into a well-oiled marketing machine.

The five automated systems working behind the scenes on your business blog:

1. RSS
2. Pings
3. Blog and RSS Directories
4. TrackBacks
5. Permalinks

RSS is both an acronym and a word. It stands for **Really Simple Syndication**.

> *RSS is used to distribute your blog content and allows you to subscribe to content from other sites automatically.*

Blogs are dynamic, and contain the ability to syndicate and publish your content because of built-in support for RSS.

NOTE: RSS is NOT a blog, but RSS is integrated into most, if not all, blog software applications. The blog publishing software automatically writes and updates your RSS file for you anytime you make a new entry to your blog.

The best thing about RSS, is that you never have to worry about managing your RSS file, which is a VERY nice thing for business owners who simply want to update their clients quickly and easily, without the hassle of waiting for their Web programmer to do it.

> The title assigned to your blog entry will be used as the title for that post in your feed. When it comes to your blog content, your feed description is pulled from your post's starting paragraph.

Your blog software will enable all posts for RSS syndication automatically, and you will find an RSS XML syndication icon that is linked to your RSS file, allowing your site content to be syndicated.

This link to your RSS file is what allows your blog content to be easily shared with other sites and to be listed in RSS feed directories.

Publishing and sharing your content becomes very easy with RSS. People who use news aggregators can receive your content directly and get notification when your blog content has been updated. They simply copy the link pointing to your RSS file and add it to their RSS news reader software.

People can receive your content right on their desktops with RSS. Voila! Bye-bye spam filters!

By leveraging the automated syndication power of RSS, you'll attract more traffic every single time you hit the PUBLISH button on your business blog!

*Blogs Are Designed To Publish, Link, And
Share Information Naturally And Instantly.*

Pings are little messages that are sent from one computer to another on the Internet.

Think of pings as your virtual sales team. They are a huge force of door-to-door sales people delivering your message to hundreds and thousands of people who want to hear from you.

On computer networks, pings are data packets that you send from one network address to another network address to see if a given computer can be reached or communicated with on that network.

Blogs use pings to send update notices to other servers when you have published something new. It's like telling everyone, "Hey, we just published some new information. Come check it out."

Here's the exciting part ...

These blogs or update servers are hunting grounds for search engine spiders. Google searches these sites, constantly visiting the links to find fresh new content. GoogleBot and other search engine spiders will find your content quickly and easily through ping updates.

Why is this important?

You Get TRAFFIC – Automatically!

You are telling all of these services that you have updated your content. They will all send their spiders to check you out and take your content back to their directories where they begin to enter your fresh content into their indexes.

No longer does Google or Yahoo! index your content within weeks and months. **Your content is indexed within hours to days – if you use blogs.**

You can expect search robots to start visiting your content within minutes of notification. This is exciting! The Web has literally become ALIVE and only blogs can keep up.

Now are you seeing why a normal, static Web site can never perform as well as a blog?

Blog and RSS Directories broadcast your content via your RSS feed far better than you ever could on your own. Submitting your blog to search directories is critical.

The good news, is that it's a one-time effort on your part, and then, it's automated from that point forward.

RSS feeds are mostly pure text and easy to crawl and index just like blogs are. Now imagine your RSS feed with keyword relevant content that links back to your blog from directories and search engines.

You have created an opportunity for exponential exposure for your blog content. Your content will now be found in more places than you could have imagined. Plus, all the content in your RSS feed links back to you.

You drive all traffic back to your blog. Your blog software automatically updates and publishes a fresh feed each time you update your blog content.

> **» BUSINESS BLOGGING SECRETS REVEALED «**
> *Google more actively visits blogs and sites with feeds it can detect because Google views RSS feeds as authoritative sources of good news and information.*

Submitting to blog and RSS directories serves to initially announce your blog. They are also sources for links, traffic, and subscribers. People search various directories looking for content to subscribe to using their RSS news aggregators. Some people search various directories looking for content to syndicate on their Web sites. Some people search these directories for new blogs to visit and lastly, you can get links from the directories themselves.

It is all about getting traffic and links back to your blog. Directories are a good start for your new blog. It is a fantastic way to promote your content.

However, you don't have to submit to every possible directory available. The more exposure you get the better, of course, but we don't want you to think that you need to submit to every known directory first in order to have good success with promoting your blog.

Popular Directories To Submit Your RSS Feed:

Feedster

http://www.feedster.com

My.Yahoo!

http://my.yahoo.com

Ping-o-matic

http://pingomatic.com/

(Automatically submits your blog to 17 individual directories with one single entry)

BlogDigger

http://www.blogdigger.com

2RSS.com

http://www.2rss.com

- Of particular interest among this group of directories is My.Yahoo.com. My.Yahoo! uses RSS feeds to create customized news delivery for individual users.
- They have an RSS search directory with hundreds of thousands of RSS feeds and growing by the multitudes every day. They are moving RSS into the mainstream and they are encouraging their users to use the RSS feeds in the My.Yahoo! directory for news and information.

Now, let's share why this piece of information is so important, and why you must register with My.Yahoo!

> **» BUSINESS BLOGGING SECRETS REVEALED «**
>
> *Register for a My.Yahoo! account today. (It's free as of this writing.) Then add your own RSS feed to your news page.*
>
> *This will cause Yahoo! to instantly go out and find your blog via your RSS feed and begin to crawl and index your blog and the Web site it's attached to. Your feed will be automatically included in the Yahoo! RSS Search directory.*
>
> *What used to take weeks and months can now be accomplished in one day for free.*
>
> *PS: You can do the same thing on your Google account home page.*

TrackBacks are necessary and a powerful component of blogging. It is like a ping, but it is a special ping. Instead of sending a notice to a blog directory or aggregation server like weblogs.com, a TrackBack sends a ping to another blog. When it pings the other blog, it writes information to that other blog about what you are writing on your blog.

This is incredible! Now, a natural back link to your blog is automatically created, simply by using the TrackBack feature.

To show you how this works in the real world, here's a practical example so you see how powerful TrackBacks are.

Imagine you're surfing the net looking for real estate investment tips. You come across a great blog post with statistics that you'd like to quote on your own blog.

In the blogosphere this is not only perfectly acceptable, it's encouraged, provided you give credit to the original author. With TrackBacks this process is a snap!

Here's how TrackBacks works…

Most blog-software applications have a TrackBack feature that creates a TrackBack URL for every post you publish.

When you are on the real estate investment blog, look for the TrackBack URL on the post you want to reference. It's normally located towards the end of a blog post, just above the comments.

You copy the TrackBack URL and enter it into the required field on your own blog post. Once you hit the publish button for your article, your blog will send a TrackBack ping to the referenced blog site.

What the TrackBack then does is write the title of your article with an excerpt from the post you just published into the comments section of the article on the referenced blog.

NOTE: There is etiquette for you to keep in mind. Only use the TrackBack feature for related posts when you want to notify the other blogger that you are talking about something he/she wrote. Make your post relevant and mention the blog article in your post by referencing it in some way.

<u>**Permalinks**</u> are exactly what the name implies. It's a permanent link! Every time you hit the publish button and create a new post, that post is assigned its own permanent and direct URL. It never changes as long as your blog is live.

> **» BUSINESS BLOGGING SECRETS REVEALED «**
>
> *Permalinks also do something else for you. Another result of permalinks is that your pages become stand-alone Web pages as well. What you have is the ability to isolate your content down to a single page of tightly focused and keyword rich content that stands out to the search engines. This is a great search engine boost for you – your content becomes much easier to index. It's one reason why search engines love blogs.*

Without permalinks there would be no way for your readers to reference and share a specific post. Instead, they would have to link to the home page of the blog and hope the person they're sending could find the specific post. Permalinks eliminate this hassle.

> **» BUSINESS BLOGGING SECRETS REVEALED «**
>
> *Permalinks are an extremely viral component of blogs and a powerful blog- promotion strategy. Other blogs using your permalinks provide a permanent reference to your blog and blog post.*
>
> *Unlike static Web pages that tend to deliver the 404 error more often than you would like, blog posts by nature never change or go away.*

Now that you've got a good feel for how a business blog works both in front of and behind the curtain, let's take a look at how you set yourself up for long-term success.

Planning For Long Term Success

chapter seven

"Good fortune is what happens when opportunity meets with planning."

– *Thomas Edison*

» The best Indy 500 race I ever saw had my partner and I standing in our seats hooting and hollering in hopes that rookie racer, Danica Patrick, would win as she worked her way up, lap by lap, to the lead position and was holding onto the lead during the final 12 laps of the race.

The buildup that had over 350,000 fans in the stadium on their feet, waving their caps, saluting Danica, as she took the lead with 11 laps to go, came as a result of what happened earlier in the race.

Excited and revved up to not only be racing 229 mph on the famous Rahal Letterman Racing Team, but on May 29, 2005, twenty-three-year-old Danica Patrick had also just made history as the first female driver to lead a lap at the Indy 500!

Chapter Seven

Then it happened.

Danica's car stalled as she tried racing out of a quick pitstop, halfway through the 500-mile race, dropping her to the back of the long line up of racers.

What a setback.

Or so it would seem. Uplifting her spirits from the embarrassment of the world watching her mishap, her championship coach, Bobby Rahall, encouraged Danica through the headset under her helmet by revealing he had also stalled out in an Indy 500 race – a common rookie mistake. Keep on going.

With all the obstacles Danica overcame throughout the race, she continued to recover, regained her composure, stayed focused and got right back on track.

Shortly after reclaiming a spot in the Top 10, Patrick spun on a caution lap, getting into an accident that damaged the nose and front wing of her car.

Ouch! Another major setback. She's out this time, right?

Nope. Her pit crew promptly made repairs, and due to the subsequent yellow flag that caused all the other drivers in the race to hold their positions, she was able to rejoin having lost only one place.

Inching her way back up, passing one car at a time, the team feared she lost her lead forever that day. But when the other race leaders pitted for fuel on lap 172, Danica made a gutsy decision, analyzed and approved by her coach, Bobby Rahall.

Danica decided to skip the last pit stop to refuel.

Planning For Long Term Success | 101

It was a risky and bold move; however, it proved to be the perfect move that got her back up to first place again from tenth, putting her in the lead for another record-breaking ten laps.

Ultimately, she ended her race in fourth place. Not bad for a rookie!

A race I'll remember forever – along with millions of others. She broke multiple records that Memorial Day weekend, and will go down in racing immortality for her performance and the records she broke that day. All that she gained that day was a result of her having a plan, perfecting her skill, and staying in the game – regardless of what came her way at three hundred miles per hour.

Ultimately, she finished 12th in the IRL IndyCar Series Championship, with 325 points, and won rookie of the year in the IRL circuit. Hats off to Danica Patrick.

Just like getting to the Indy 500 championship takes a lot of planning and preparation, winning with New Media also takes a lot of planning and preparation.

The Indy 500 race is famous for being a very difficult track, and a very long race. So, if you're not in it for the long-haul, you won't take the lead without a properly executed plan.

Your business blog plays an important role when marketing with the New Media. To use it effectively, you need to know exactly how to start, maintain, and leverage your blog for ongoing benefits to your business.

For a blog to be effective, it must be well planned, well written, well organized, and well marketed. Unfortunately, we see far too many business owners stalling on the starting line and wondering why they're not getting the results they wanted.

Or they meet an obstacle on the track, and think it's over for them.

The fact is that your success with buzz, branding, connection, and profits starts with a **Strategic Business Blogging Plan**.

As part of the BLOG Interactive 360™ New Media Marketing system, we've used our 4,000+ hours of research, coaching, and consulting experience on blogs and New Media to develop an intense 35-page planning playbook.

This proven process has helped hundreds of business owners around the world quickly and simply develop a winning plan. A plan that links their business blogging to their New Media Strategy, and integrates it with their overall company marketing plan.

If you're serious about eliminating needless trial and error, and successfully integrating your business blogging for long-term results, you can check out that program at BLOGinteractive360.com.

For now, let's get you started with some of the most important questions you'll need to answer before starting your business blog.

One note of coaching advice: Don't cheat yourself by answering with a one-sentence reply. Grab a notebook or journal and capture your detailed answers in writing.

WHAT RESULTS DO YOU WANT FROM YOUR BLOG?

Simply answering with "more traffic" or "more subscribers" is not going to help you in any way. Be specific, and far-reaching with your goals.

- How do you want your blog to support your objectives?
- Do you want to attract prospects to a specific product or service? Or to your company as a whole?

- ❏ Do you want to provide customer support for an existing product line?
- ❏ How about public relations for you within your profession or industry?
- ❏ Do you want to create buzz by stirring up controversy through opinionated reviews of industry news?

Knowing what your most desired response is will help you define the context for your content. Blogs accelerate online communication, help build reputation, promote information sharing, and amplify the connectedness of the Internet.

Who Is Your Target Audience?

To know your audience is to know what they need, want, and desire. Your blog must provide value to your audience. If you want it to be effective in creating a dialogue, you'll need to talk about things that are relevant to them. That's what will bring you repeat visits.

Taking the time now to define your target market and the people who make up your audience will give you three important advantages:

1. It will help you define what your target audience is looking for
2. It will give you the information you need to intelligently blend your style with their needs, wants, and desires
3. It will keep you on track, focused and motivated in your blogging posts (one of the greatest challenges for new bloggers)

Your purpose and intention in this planning process is not so much to impress your ideal audience. Rather it is to keep from offending them.

People will be forgiving if you occasionally go off-track, but they won't be as understanding if you offend them. (We'll talk more about how to avoid doing that in section three of this book.)

Who <u>specifically</u> is your target audience? Who will you be speaking to?

- Professionals?
- Enthusiasts/hobbyists?
- People in a specific industry?
- General population?
- A certain age group?
- People of a specific ethnic background?
- People who have spiritual or religious beliefs?
- A political audience?

Identifying your target audience will help you keep your message on the mark and effective. Reliable results come when you use your passion to blog or publish relevant information for a like-minded community of people. To deliver relevant information, you need to know their wants needs, and desires.

Who Should Run Your Business Blog?

You have three choices when it comes to choosing who will run your business blog.

1. You can blog yourself
2. You can have one of your company team members blog
3. You can hire a professional

If you're going to create the content for your business blog yourself, there's only one thing you must have if you are to be successful with your blog – PASSION!

If you don't have passion, then you can expect your blog experience to be less than exciting. Eventually you will abandon your blog and your audience.

If you have a passionate interest in something and the burning desire to converse regularly on that topic, you'll have the strength to go forward.

If you have something to say, something to sell, or something to socialize, then a blog is a great way to get your message out there. Ultimately, to make the best use of your blog for promoting your personal or business messages, you must be willing to commit to developing relationships and content that interests your target audience.

A consistent flow of information and content is what keeps the search engines returning to your blog. It is what builds an audience and keeps them returning to your blog and it is the only way to make use of blogs.

You don't need to post multiple times each day, and you don't even need to post every day. We've seen clients get awesome results with three regular posts per week.

Depending on your niche, you might be like one of our clients who got national exposure with CNN Money and The Wall Street Journal thanks to just three blog posts on three cross-referenced blogs.

When it comes to the conversation part of business blogging, it takes time to build an audience who trusts you. If you can accept that and you can take a long-term view of blogging, then you can expect success and good results in a much *shorter* time span. As opposed to rushing out for immediate results, only to stall out in the pits, due to your surge of excited energy when you first start out, but without the right moves to keep it going.

Many of our larger and more successful clients don't have the time to blog personally themselves. We've worked with them to coach one or two team members who are passionate about their company's niche, specialty, or industry – and they love it! The business owner is happy. The team member has fun, and the business gets the traffic, buzz, and branding it deserves.

On a political campaign, it's almost never the candidate who regularly blogs. We always coach at least two full-time members of the campaign team to follow the system. The candidate and part-timers can all contribute to the blog, but the consistency is always guaranteed by the full-timers who have the responsibility.

The third alternative for business owners is hiring a professional. There are a number of companies that offer content creation services for businesses wishing to incorporate blogging into their overall marketing strategy. Proper planning, agreement on schedules and goals, and finding a professional with a "voice" (character) that matches the owner or the company image is essential if you pursue this route.

Note: If you do hire a professional to create content for your business blog, NEVER make that person someone they're not. You never want to hire an outsider who blogs under the name of the company owner. You will get found out, and your readers and customers will feel betrayed.

The Bottom Line

Don't just start a business blog because it's been effective in getting other people incredible results. That's not enough to sustain your efforts and get results yourself.

Establish a plan for your business blog. Link it with your complete New Media Marketing Strategy, then integrate that with the overall marketing plan of your company.

Be unique.

Feel free to examine the blogs that contain topics and features that appeal to you. Build your own ideas from the observations of reading other blogs. Add your own unique spin as you generate ideas for your blog. Taking the time to do these things now will provide focus and direction as you move forward, starting your own blog.

ROI vs. Your "Business Blogging Budget"

A common question we get from our business coaching clients about marketing with business blogs and other New Media tools like Podcasts is on the Return on Investment. This is a personal question that is unique to your industry and business goals, and it's one that requires significant analysis to determine what metrics you'll need to track.

For now, let me share something with you to help you budget your time, money, and effort in regards to your business blogging. It's a law that should be the #1 determining factor in determining budgeting parameters for all your online and offline marketing.

That law is …

Know the Lifetime Value of your Clients

Lifetime Value (LTV) is a term that sadly many business owners have never heard. And if they have heard about it, they don't understand how to calculate this crucial figure and how to put it to use to literally squash the competition.

Let's do a simple overview of LTV and then we'll relate it to your business blogging and New Media Marketing.

Lifetime Value Defined By Example

LTV is defined as the total dollar amount your average client purchases over the entire period (life) that they're likely to do business with you.

You can use actual sales figures from past years to arrive at an exact figure, or you can estimate. Either way there are a number of strategies for making your estimates more accurate. To give you a clearer picture, I'll share an example using actual historical numbers.

Let's say that you've determined that your repeat customers stay with you an average of three years and you currently have 300 loyal customers. Your net profits over the past three years totals $780,000. The Lifetime Value = $780,000/300 or $2,600!

Each new client you can get and keep is worth an average of $2,600 net profit to you over the average client life of three years.

Now, here's why lifetime value is so important and how you can use it to outfox your competition in your offline and online marketing. Let's start with an offline example since that will probably be a bit more familiar to most brick-and-mortar businesses.

How To Use LTV To Improve Your Offline Marketing

As an example, let's say you run an ad in a professional publication that costs $1,000 and you get 35 sales at $25 per sale. That's a total revenue of $875 (35 sales X $25 each). On the surface that doesn't even appear to even cover your costs. Most businesses would consider these results a failure. Once you understand how to apply the LTV principle, you will see it quite differently.

Instead, you'll see that for every $28.57 per client you invest ($1,000 ad yields 35 clients) – you get a $2,600 return, and that's not even counting on improving your service or product to increase purchase frequency or the amount of time a client stays with you!

I don't know about you, but I'll take as many new clients like that as you can find me!

Now THAT is thinking and working smarter, not harder.

How To Use LTV To Improve Your Online Marketing With Business Blogs

One of the biggest hurdles that business owners need to overcome when it comes to marketing with business blogs and New Media is the amount of time they think it will take.

It's a real concern and something that needs to be addressed objectively using real data, not subjectively by "feeling" or "thinking." This is where knowing and understanding the LTV of your clients presents itself as an indispensable tool.

Let's continue with the example from above, and assume that your LTV is $2,600. Let's say that you're real conservative in estimating the returns you'll get from marketing with business blogs, say an average of two new clients per month in the coming year. That means you can spend up to $5,200 (in time or money) each month to get those clients and breakeven.

We know you don't want to just break-even, you want to make a profit on every client you bring in.

So, let's just take one quarter of that total and say that your business blogging budget would be $1,300 per month. If it's your actual personal time that will be dedicated to business blogging, and you value an hour of your time at $100, you can start by budgeting 13 hours per month for your business blogging efforts.

If it's actual hard cash that you have to pay to an outsource agent or someone on your staff, you now have a numerical benchmark to make things simple. WOW – pretty cool, huh!!!

Successful Budgeting Rooted In Simplicity

The reason we're so passionate about this principle is simple. It can literally transform your business or professional practice into a client-focused, profit-producing powerhouse!

Among the many practical applications this law has, it has a powerful intangible impact on your philosophy of doing business. It will free you to give more to your clients than they expect. Plus you will never feel that you are losing money when you offer promotions or FREE products or offers.

In 1992, when my business coach showed me this powerful principle, I was blown away. It literally revolutionized my approach to marketing and customer service. It prompted me to maximize my marketing by going online with a business that delivered 100% of its services offline. It significantly boosted our profits and left our competitors dazed and confused. I'd like the same for you.

I can guarantee you that once you realize clients are actually an ongoing revenue source rather than just part of "today's sales," you'll reap a profit windfall, while at the same time exceeding your clients' expectations.

When you combine the understanding of Lifetime Value with the online marketing methods of business blogging, Podcasts, and leveraging social networks, you'll have a huge advantage over your competitors in the New Media Marketplace.

Make Your Blogging Fast, Easy And Fun With The Best Software For Your Unique Needs

chapter eight

Jill: A pressurized window washer? It shattered a window!
Tim: Every piece was clean though, all of them.

- From the hit TV show, Home Improvement

≫ Blog software is any software that allows you to publish content with a blog. Clean, simple, and easy!

There...chapter done! Next!

OK, seriously now…

As you look around to get started with your first business blog, it may seem as if there's a confusing number of blog software programs to choose for your business blog.

Sure, there may be dozens of companies out there who have some comparative variations in their features. When it comes down to it though, there are really only two types of blogging software options:

1. Self-hosted blog software

2. Third-party-hosted blog software

When you're looking to maximize ALL the social, buzz, and search engine benefits that come with business blog and New Media marketing – there is one winner hands down.

1. Self-Hosted Blog Software

Self-hosted blog software requires you or a programmer to download, install, and configure the blog software on your own server or domain account using your own Web site hosting provider.

Three examples are:

- WordPress (www.wordpress.org/) – free/open source
- Greymatter (www.noahgrey.com/greysoft/) – free/open source
- Movable Type (www.sixapart.com/movabletype/) – pay per install

With self-hosted blog software, you'll need to make sure that your hosting provider meets the minimum requirements to run the blog software. That's usually not a problem – 99% of quality hosting services easily meet or exceed the basic requirements of WordPress for instance.

(If your host is one of the rare few that doesn't meet the minimum requirements, you should probably consider a new host anyway. That's a good indication there are additional antiquated systems impacting reliability that you don't know about.)

If you're like me, a control-freak, then you'll need the self-hosted option.

Self-hosted is the way to go if you want the greatest level of flexibility and control over your blog. If you're not technically inclined, you can easily hire a designer or programmer to load and configure your self-hosted WordPress blog for the price of a night out at the movies.

The Address You Want

When you host your own business blog, you can have any address you like. For example:

> http://blog.yourdomain.com
>
> http://www.yourdomain.com
>
> http://www.yourdomain.com/blog

Regardless, if you decide to put the word blog in the name of the URL you choose, it will have all the blogging bells and whistles and you'll have complete control over the keywords you choose for your domain name – provided you beat your competitor grabbing the name before he does.

The Advantages:

- #1 BIGGIE! If you host your blog on the same URL as your main Web site, all the keyword relevance and inbound links that your blog will generate will all be credited to your Web site URL. That means improved positioning in search engine results.

- Maximum flexibility on custom programming
- Complete customization of your design (including the ability to integrate seamlessly into your existing Web site template.)
- You can allocate as much storage as you like
- Extend the features of your blog with blog plug-ins (performance upgrades)

The Disadvantages:

- Self management of upgrades
- Self support
- Hiring a programmer to install and regularly update your blog *(as already mentioned though, your initial install can be done for about the cost of a night out at the movies – provided you're connected to the right resources, and you know how to manage an outsourcing agent)*

Self-Hosted Blog Recommendation:

For most business owners looking for the maximum capabilities in control, customization, and search engine optimization related to your main Web site URL – nothing beats a self-hosted blog.

The absolute, hands-down winner for this type of blog software is WordPress. The fact that it is open-source software (free for everyone to use) is another perk. With WordPress, you can set up as many internal or external business blogs as you want and never have any licensing or maintenance fees other than your regular monthly hosting fees.

Don't let the free open-source nature of WordPress fool you either. WordPress has one of the world's most active programming communities constantly working on upgrades and improvements.

From time to time, we'll upload videos to our blog at AdvancedBusinessBlogging.com to show our subscribers how to get started with WordPress, along with some of the cool features and new plug-ins that come out.

We're HUGE fans of WordPress, and utilize New Media channels to express our passion for WordPress. As a result, we'll often get to test out new beta versions to give feedback on what could be improved upon – all the privileges of networking online and utilizing New Media methods of connecting with powerful players in the blogosphere.

2. Third-Party-Hosted Blog Software Services

The second type of blog software is a blog-hosting service. Blog hosting is much the same as regular Web hosting. You simply create an account on a signup page at the third-party blog host of your choice and you can begin blogging in 15-minutes.

Third-party-hosted blog service-providers supply you with blog publishing software on their servers. You simply sign up with them to set up a blog account.

You aren't required to install any software or get a separate Web site hosting account or domain name. Some examples of third-party hosted blog providers would be:

- BlogHarbor (www.blogharbor.com)
- TypePad (www.typepad.com)
- Squarespace (www.squarespace.com)

This is the quickest and easiest way for the average person to start blogging. If you have no experience with uploading files to your own Web site, or if you don't want to deal with hiring a programmer, this is an attractive option.

Once you are signed up, you are given a blog address similar to an address like this: http://myblogname.blogserviceprovider.com/. Some hosted service-providers support domain mapping that enables you to use http://www.myblogname.com as a redirect.

Some services offer a free version of paid accounts that have limited features. Some free accounts are trial accounts, so check to make sure you are registered for the right type of account.

The Advantages:

- Signing up and getting started is a snap
- No software installation or configuration required
- Host managed software upgrades
- Host provided support

The Disadvantages:

- Limited customization and control
- Limited bandwidth and storage
- Monthly subscription fee for hosting

> **》BUSINESS BLOGGING SECRETS REVEALED《**
>
> - *Another serious disadvantage to consider has to do with search engine optimization. If one of your goals is to associate good keyword ranking and inbound links with your main Web site URL, then a third-party-hosted blog will not help you anywhere close to what a self-hosted blog can do for you. That's because any keyword relevancy and inbound links credited to your third-party-hosted blog do not flow over to your main Web site.* ☹

Third-Party-Hosted Recommendations:

Most blogging tools provide adequate trial periods. If you're serious about marketing with blogs and New Media – free blog hosting services like Blogger.com is not an option.

If you must host your blog using the third-party option, we recommend BlogHarbor.com for third-party hosting of your business blog. From our research and surveying we've found the customer support for BlogHarbor is superb, and we have some friends who use this for their main blog, and love it.

BlogHarbor is a great service that is very easy to use yet very nicely designed for serious content management. BlogHarbor is fast becoming a platform of choice for serious bloggers and content publishers.

In fact, they have the best blog stats we've seen for a hosted service. You get metrics on HTML requests, RSS requests, unique hosts served, most popular categories, most popular articles, most commented articles and, of course, referrer stats.

BlogHarbor allows you to publish HTML pages right along with your blog and maintain a consistent look and feel across your entire site. This is a very good system. They provide a dynamic feed for each category you create, and they provide you with an enormous amount of storage space and bandwidth.

One really nice feature that BlogHarbor offers is an email subscription for people in your audience who don't yet use RSS for getting content updates, but want to stay in touch with you.

Email updates for your content is supported and built right into your BlogHarbor software system. They also offer secured channels and user/group management for rights-based access to content and they also provide automatic Podcasting.

Just like WordPress, you simply add your audio/media attachment to your post and when it is syndicated, BlogHarbor automatically adds the RSS element tag to it so that media aggregators can receive your Podcast. These are a few of the highlights for BlogHarbor.

TypePad is another third-party hosting service where you get less space and bandwidth than you do with BlogHarbor, but you get a brand leader. TypePad was created by SixApart; the creator of the server-based blog software, Movable Type. They're considered by many to be the leaders in the third-party hosted blog software category.

» COACHES SECRET REVEALED «

We do feel we need to reveal the fact that we recommend our private consulting clients use WordPress to create and host their business blog

– for a variety of reasons. Ninety-nine out of 100 times, we'll steer our clients toward the self-hosted option above any other third-party hosting option available.

The Final Decision

Our advice and bias for business owners is clear, but choosing the best one is really based on what you want to accomplish with your blog. You need to consider how much time and money you're willing to invest compared to your long-range goals for your business.

Choosing to make things fast and simple right now could end up costing you a lot more money down the road if you need to move your blog because you're not getting the search engine rankings you had hoped for your main sales or campaign Web site.

We see this happen all too often with clients who find our course secrets too late. So – now you know. Don't say you weren't warned.

» **BONUS COACHING TIP:** *Advanced business blog management software for your desktop*

Desktop blog editors allow you to remotely manage one or more blogs, which will save you time and allow you to easily develop, publish, and manage all of your blog content locally on your hard drive.

These tools are NOT mini-blogs that run on your hard drive, although we've seen an application or two that work along those lines.

What we're referring to here are tools that are really text editors for bloggers. When you want to perform word processing tasks on a

Windows computer, you normally fire up Microsoft Word or some other word processor to create your document. A blog editor allows you compose and publish your blog content from your desktop in the same way.

Three Benefits Of Using A Desktop Blog Editor

1. The first and immediate benefit is convenience.

It's much more convenient to publish with a desktop tool instead of firing up your Web browser, logging into your blog software control panel, and then accessing your Web-based text editor every time you want to publish. While publishing from the administration area on your blog software is very easy, you can still benefit from a client-based tool.

2. The next benefit of a client-based blog tool is local and remote content management.

A client-based blog publishing tool will allow you to remotely manage and edit your posts. You can easily manage your content locally by saving drafts to your local computer while you develop your content for publishing. You don't have to be connected to the Internet to do this. You can save your work when you're not finished yet, but need to get to the gym, or when you're just not ready to publish a particular post.

Then, when you're back from the gym, or ready to let your readers see what you just wrote, you simply open up the item you were last working on in your blog editor and push a button to publish to your server. Voila! Done!

You can also remotely view items you've published in the past and modify them. A blog editor allows you to format your content with the ease and familiarity of a standard word-processor application.

3. *A final benefit we want to point out is multiple blog management. If you are publishing more than one blog, consider using a desktop blog editor.*

You can easily configure a blog editor to manage all of your blogs. All you have to do is enter the same information you use to log into your blog-server tool along with the specific type of server software you are using and your blog editor will keep that information as part of its configuration.

To use your blog editor, you simply open the program, select the profile for the blog you want to publish to, and you are on your way.

When you're finished, just log out of that profile, and log on to another one of your business blogs, or log out entirely. This is a very simple process and a fantastic time saver.

Most blog editors support most of the popular server-installed and blog-hosted software tools available and also support custom configuration for blog software not directly supported. Check to make sure that your blog tool is supported before you purchase a desktop blog editor.

CONTENT THAT CREATES RAVING FANS

chapter nine

As Dorothy, the Scarecrow, and the Tin Man join hands and skip together "to Oz," they enter a thick forest which immediately spooks and frightens Dorothy.

Dorothy: *"I don't like this forest. It's dark and creepy...Do you suppose we'll meet any wild animals?"*

Worried that they will be attacked, the Tin Woodsman predicts the dark forest will be filled mostly with "lions and tigers and bears."

Dorothy: *Lions?*
Scarecrow: *And tigers?*
Tin Man: *And bears!*
Dorothy: *Lions and tigers and bears, oh my!*

– *From the movie,* The Wizard of Oz

Chapter Nine

»When you're venturing out into the new territory of marketing with your business blog, you may not have to deal with lions, and tigers, and bears. However, you do need to simultaneously attract people and spiders and crawlers.

People and spiders and crawlers, Oh my! What's a new business blogger to do?

When most people start marketing their business with blogs they may feel like Dorothy trying to reach the Emerald City in the Wizard of Oz. The only difference is they don't have a yellow brick road to follow.

But now you do!

In the following two chapters we'll get you on track to serious results with both people and search engines. This chapter will cover people, and Chapter 9.5 will cover those search engine spiders that we marketers love.

Before we get to either, it's important to take the time to dispel a few dangerous fairytale myths with the facts.

The Web Marketing Fairytale

More and more business owners are starting blogs every day. Many are doing it with the goal of getting better search engine rankings to bring more targeted traffic to their Web site, and with that, more exposure for their company.

Not a bad goal, but as they try to achieve it, many think just posting content that their target audience is passionate about is all that's required.

Not true.

Even more people fall prey to the belief that postings made everyday packed with good keywords alone will bring them the results that want.

They still believe the Web Marketing 1.0 fairytale that high quality content doesn't matter to get meaningful traffic.

Unfortunately, that's not the way to Oz, it's not the way back home to Kansas, and it's certainly not the way to effectively position your business blog as the centerpiece of your New Media Marketing Strategy.

Producing content that way will never help you attract the people you want as regular readers of your blog. Without people who turn into raving fans, you'll never get the viral impact and valuable inbound links that you want.

Fortunately, the yellow brick road to business blogging success (with both people and spiders) is not that hard to find. And it's surprisingly easy-to-follow once you're on it.

Gaining popularity with both people and search engine spiders really becomes an intuitive part of the process.

Why? Because a well-structured blog is naturally attractive to both people and search engine spiders alike. The way a blog is structured and maintained gives these two key players exactly what they want most.

Why People Like Blogs

As we've mentioned in Section One of this book, blogs are a technological extension of the natural drive that people have to connect, contribute, and communicate. Blogs are rapidly becoming more and more popular with people for three main reasons.

1. They're Topical Which Means They Save Time

A good blog is topical and is run by someone who's passionate about that niche or viewpoint. Because of that passion, those blog owners act as a filter for the vast amount of information that's available both online and offline today. That filtering, analysis, and yes — even opinionated commenting, is valuable to people who share an interest in that same area.

The filtering saves time, and the topical focus adds immediate relevant value to people who share the same worldview or perspective.

The thinking behind this natural influencer is that people trust that if you're a lot like them, and you recommend something that you enjoy, chances are, they're going to like it too – because your interests are so similar.

Statistically, only 14% of the population actually enjoys doing research and statistical analysis – just for the fun of it. So, if you can do the research in your industry for your readers, they'll quickly become fans of your blog. More importantly, they'll become loyal fans of you personally, because you save them a ton of time and energy that allows them to focus on what they do best.

2. Active Interaction

Blogs have the built-in capability to allow your readers to instantly communicate with you. The interaction capability built into blogging software (through commenting and TrackBacks) makes it easy for the reader to engage in the conversation. They get to share their comments and thoughts immediately in reaction to what they just read.

This active interaction opens the dialogue and makes them feel part of the process. They're no longer just passive consumers of information (like they would feel at a normal Web site) – now they're active participants.

Everyone loves to add their two cents; some prefer to add their two dollars. What I like most about this aspect of what blogs offer, is that you'll develop deep connections that lead to real friendships with your loyal fans who join in the discussion and contribute valuable content.

I can think of numerous people I've met through our blogs, who I admire due to what they contribute to the conversation.

3. *Connection*

Blogs work best when they are tightly focused on a specific niche. People want to be connected with like-minded individuals. So when a person with similar interests finds your blog and likes what you have to say, they begin forming a connection with you.

As you deliver more and more targeted content, that connection deepens and expands into credibility and trust. You win. They win. Your business blog is the medium that makes it happen.

We've developed some of the most successful strategic partnerships with people who started out as blog readers, who turned into raving fans and who have since then been promoting our BLOG Interactive 360 Course to their list ever since. All as a direct result of connecting online, sharing similar interests with a passion for business blogging as the core.

Once they took the next step, from being a blog reader, to participating in one of our online interactive courses, they saw the value it gave their own business and became raving fans.

Now they tell all their friends and clients about the course! Naturally, we like to thank them by granting them strategic partnership status with generous profit sharing checks each month.

It's a beautiful business friendship! There's nothing like doing business with people you enjoy hanging out with as well.

Why Search Engine Spiders Love Blogs

Unlike normal Web sites, your business blog won't need "black hat" tactics and complex code revisions to get good search engine rankings.

You could say that business blogs were born for search engine optimization. The very construction and activity of a blog is naturally attractive for search engine spiders.

The reasons why a good business blog is prime food for search engine spiders are remarkably similar to the top three reasons that people like blogs. They are:

1. Topical Relevance

The only purpose of the search engine is to find content that is highly relevant to keywords entered. When your business blog is tightly focused in a specific niche area, your relevancy is likely to be naturally high with relatively little effort on your part.

Why? Because when you know what your keywords are and you produce content that stays focused on your niche area, peppering your posts with your keywords almost becomes an unconscious act. Your relevancy and rankings shoot up as you produce more and more content that is directly relevant to your keywords.

Knowing that the job of search engines is to provide relevant content allows you to naturally place your business blog content on a banquet table where search engine spiders are eager to feast.

2. Frequent Activity

Search engines are designed to not only deliver relevant content, but also the newest, freshest information available. Search engine users want the most up-to-date information possible. Since blogging software allows for instant publishing to the Internet, those blog based Web sites are frequently updated.

Well-planned business blogs by their very nature have both the relevancy and the highly active posting frequency that search engine spiders want. Hence, those crawlers and spiders will return to your site more and more as your frequency increases. As those visits take place over and over again (with your topical relevancy remaining constant), your search engine rankings continue to climb.

Frequent additions of new information + relevant content = activity that search engine spiders can't help but be addicted to and want to visit again and again.

3. *Links And Connection*

Just like people like to be connected, search engine spiders like to be connected too, only in a different way. Most search engine algorithms love links, especially Google. The more relevant links you have in your blog, or to your blog, the more value search engines give you as a connection point to more relevant content their users are looking for.

Blogs are built to connect to each other. Since bloggers are often referencing each other (either through TrackBacks or direct links,) inbound links can be generated very quickly. Even better yet, those inbound links have increased value because they're often from sites that have a natural relevance to your site's topical content.

The true basis for linking power comes from the fact that your content is valuable enough to have people who want to link to your posts/articles. Without good quality content that people want to link to or reference, you can make keyword dense posts as frequently as you want, but you'll always get sub par search engine results.

Although the frequency of posting undeniably helps, it's not a magic wand. Overall, quality of content trumps frequency in most niche areas. Assuming of course, that posts are made consistently and stay on topic — both people and spiders will devour the content to create a powerful linking connection.

The answer to remarkable search engine rankings in your chosen niche AND permeating popularity with people is right in front of your face. It's right in your blogging software, and it's right inside you.

Much like the scarecrow, the tin man, and the lion who were told by the Wizard of Oz that they always had what they sought, you'll find that most of what you're looking for can already be found in your business and life.

- Like the scarecrow you need to use your brain to properly plan and organize your business blog with a specific target niche.

- Like the tin man, you need to have your heart in your business blog and be passionate about what you're blogging about.

- And like the lion, you have to be courageous enough to just step out there and start doing it.

When you take your brain, your heart, and your courage and you add it to your business blog – you'll be well on your way to optimizing your marketing with both people and search engine spiders alike.

Creating Content People Will Love

Since people are our primary focus with all marketing, remember that all the top search engine rankings in the world will not build rapport and relationships with your target audience.

7 Coaching Tips To Build Powerful Relationships Online:

These seven coaching tips will give you a jump-start, creating content that builds relationships. You'll be able to use these seven tips as a framework for successfully developing your own personal style with experience.

1. Communicate With Authenticity

Your communication must be authentic. When you blog or publish content, let your true self come through. Blogs are by nature personal and up close in communication. You must let your authentic voice come through. Each blog will be unique because each publisher is unique. Whatever the topic you are blogging about make sure you inject your personality into your writing.

In order to create loyal readership, visitors must come to trust you and feel like they know you in some way. It doesn't mean that they need to know all your personal details, but you do need to connect with your audience in a very real way. Keep it simple by working with your strengths and natural style. (We've got some awesome coaching that'll give you major head start in Section Three of this book.)

2. Establish Credibility

Your content must be credible and authoritative. Your credibility will rest largely with the "voice" of your blog, that is, your authenticity. Some individuals and businesses bring a level of credibility to the Web and have a built-in audience. For most however, credibility is built over time.

As you begin to publish content that is found to be of high value and useful by others, you begin to build authority. When your audience comes to believe in the value of your content, you'll be building credibility and authority. They will look to you and seek your opinion and advice. These are some of the key factors you will need to build your brand and your reputation online.

Blogs are fantastic reputation builders. What better way to have automated blog promotion and blog marketing activities than with other people who will link to you and reference you without you having to ask?

You can build your audience exponentially when you get other blogs to reference your blog content and send you traffic. Blogging has given rise to what some are calling news masters. Some bloggers are in the business of referencing relevant news, facts, information, and content of various kinds that they find useful; and, when they find something of value to their audience, they talk about it or blog it (this is what's referred to as blogging).

Each reference you get to your content can lead to a multitude of additional references as more people who find their way to you also turn around and link to you as well.

Bloggers act as a filter. When people find a blog that is useful they will link to it and refer others to it. You can become the authority within your niche. Others will look to you to filter the news for them on what is valuable and newsworthy.

> **» BUSINESS BLOGGING SECRETS REVEALED «**
>
> *Your content builds your reputation with Google. As more people link to you, your blog credibility builds your reputation as more people read it and reward you with repeat visits.*
>
> *As you learn how to blog, remember you are building credibility, authority and reputation.*

3. Publish With Consistency

You must publish fresh content regularly. A stale blog will not generate traffic from the search engines and it will have visitors leaving your blog like crazy.

You want to capture "mindshare" of your ideal audience before your competitor does. Then hold on to it. Otherwise, one of the sharks swimming outside your tank will want to capture anyone who jumps out as a result of being disappointed, when you don't feed them regularly on the subjects they seek to know more about.

If you aren't up to the task of publishing on a regular schedule of at least once per week, then one of the following may give you the solution you need:

1. Prepare your posts ahead of time; then publish on a specific schedule

2. Get someone on your team to write and publish

3. Hire a professional blogger to do it for you

Number two and three are straightforward delegation. Number one involves leveraging software to increase your efficiency.

There are some stand-alone software programs that handle scheduled posting very effectively. This is a little more advanced, so we won't go into too much detail here.

We wanted to mention this since we recognize that many people are very interested in buzz and branding power of marketing with blogs, but they have scheduling challenges or travel too unpredictably to meet any type of strict writing schedule.

These software programs allow the option to post to the future or "schedule" your posts. This lets you manage your time by planning your content ahead of time and then publishing it at a future date/time.

Some blog software programs like WordPress have some functionality of these stand-alone programs built right in.

4. Link To Reference Sources.

Link to relevant supporting research and facts to boost the level of importance for the points you are making. At the heart of all Internet activity is "search." People like to find stuff! We search for stuff all the time.

Pay attention to how you feel when you read content that references other great content. You get a sense of discovery and you feel smart for having found it by being at the right blog at the right time.

Help your readers find stuff that gives them more reasons to trust you and get addicted to your stuff. No matter what you publish, link out to other content if it's relevant. That helps your search engine rankings and your readers.

Take advantage of the growing obsession we all seem to have with "saving time." This is the main reason why RSS feeds are powerful. They help people subscribe to great content without having to hunt for it through a gazillion individual Web sites.

Help people save time by being an authoritative and trusted source of filtered news and high value content.

5. Open Comments And Allow TrackBacks.

In your blog software, you will have the option to turn on or off the commenting and TrackBack features. Turn on comments and TrackBacks so that you can develop a dialogue with your readers and allow other blogs to ping-reference your content.

If you want to connect with your audience with content that will move them – or move them to take action – you need to allow them the means to talk back to you. When you give people the opportunities to react to your content, you allow them to connect even deeper with your content.

This is powerful.

6. Niche It.

Being a generalist or creating content for a broad audience will never be as profitable as content creation for a specific niche. Your richest returns will come from targeting a niche market, topic, or theme, and focus on the informational needs of individuals in that market.

Focusing on a niche will allow you to tighten your message and keep your content relevant.

A blog that builds reputation around a theme will need to be more on topic with each published item. General rambling isn't as productive.

A themed or topical blog publishes content that doesn't move away from the central theme; however, it can touch on any and all related information that would assist in reaching and relating to an audience.

7. Connect Personally

As a New Media Marketing tool, blogs allow you to reach out to a much larger audience within your niche than you'd ever be able to with conventional Web marketing methods.

As you begin to harness the power of the New Media Marketplace, you'll appreciate how powerful blogs are at transmitting your message to far-reaching audiences who are interested and looking for what you have to offer. It may start with great content, but that content must not only capture attention and inform, it must also connect with people personally.

To do this you have to imagine that you're having a conversation with just one person at a time. This conversation is where you connect on a personal level in a way that encourages your audience to move from stranger to friend. Only then can you build the relationship from friend to customer, then customer to raving fan.

It is possible to communicate, but not connect, with your business blog. If you focus on having one single conversation at a time, you'll almost guarantee your success in connecting with your ideal audience.

Invite reader feedback and participation as if you were writing an email, expecting them to reply. Leave your post with a lingering question that begs to be answered or challenged.

Practice these seven start-up strategies for creating content that turns people into raving fans. Then get ready to turn those all-important search engine spiders into raving fans!

Laying Out The Spider Bait

chapter 9.5

> *Dr. Otto Octavius: [grabs Peter with a tentacle] "I want you to find your friend Spider-Man. Tell him to meet me at the Westside Tower at 3 o'clock."*
>
> – Spider-Man II, The Movie

≫ In the previous chapter, you saw how to use your business blog content to attract crowds of raving fans to your site. In this chapter, we'll reveal how to get those all-important search engine spiders to show up more often to crawl all over your content, and drive your rankings up the charts.

Harnessing The Organic Search Properties Of Blogs

Your business blog will get rankings through what you write. Search engines will only index what you publish. You must know your niche, know your keywords and publish information that informs your market niche and answers their needs.

Due to the organic keyword generation that takes place with a well-focused business blog, you'll pull in traffic from places you'd never imagine.

Sometimes the bait was within your own content all the time, but you just didn't see what the search engines saw until someone typed in a "natural" search phrase that just happened to be found within your content.

When you see this happening for keyword phrases on a regular basis (we'll show you how to find this information later in this chapter), it means there's a possible keyword focus worth exploring. Blogs have a way of highlighting little nuggets of opportunities like this because of how powerful organic indexing works.

You don't have to work hard at trying to manipulate the process. You simply have to work at developing great content that's keyword focused, and stick to your plan. Anything more than that is mechanical and distracting and will detract from the blogging process.

What Is Search Engine Optimization?

A well written, niche focused, and properly structured business blog will create a traffic bonanza of high-quality visitors. Before we go any further with strategies and tactics to boost your search engine ranking, let's make sure that we're all on the same page with what search engine optimization (SEO) is.

SEO is simply getting a high enough ranking in the search engines for your keywords that your content will generate visitors to your Web site.

Compelling sites and content titles with magnetic descriptions help motivate users to click on your links in the search engine results and visit your blog.

SEO requires an optimized Web site. This is a Web site that has a structure that is attractive to search engine spiders. The spiders will visit your site and "crawl" all over your content.

While SEO spiders crawl through your content, they pick up your keywords and determine what your page is all about. The spiders then carry that information back to the search engines and your site gets "indexed" (ranked) accordingly.

When people type in the keywords that you're using on your business blog, your pages will show up in the search results. The idea is to get your pages ranked high enough to get traffic to your site.

Obviously the sites that rank in the top results, for example, in positions one through 30, draw a lot more traffic than sites ranked at 100 or 200.

Why Blogs Enhance Search Engine Marketing

In the past, only mass media and major news sites carried frequently updated content with breaking news headlines and stories. The search engine spiders would be crawling these sites continuously, because these sites were known by the search engines as sources for the freshest, newest and, therefore, most relevant content to be found on the Internet.

Now blogs are creating millions of mini-news sites with rich information and links. Bloggers update their content frequently with all types of late-breaking information. News and political blogs have outpaced mainstream media outlets in their ability to get information out to the masses faster – and all in real time.

Search engines specifically target blogs as another huge source of high value, fresh and highly relevant information and they want it as fast as you can publish it.

> *The more frequently you publish the more visits you will get from Google, Yahoo! and other search engines.*

Think about it.

Everyone wants to be the first to know something. So, if you can provide the information your audience wants – first – you'll be the one they favor, along with the search engines who want to provide the most relevant places to the masses who are searching for the NEWEST information.

Blogs get crawled often and deeply by search engine spiders. This means that you get your content indexed by Google, Yahoo!, and others *in mere hours or days* instead of weeks or months.

You no longer need to go to Google or Yahoo!, to submit your site, and then wait for two-to-three months before you start to see yourself showing up among the rankings. Nope – that's old school, Web Marketing 1.0.

Why does this happen? Search engines are in the business of delivering the most accurate and relevant information as possible in their search results. They know that if they don't deliver relevant content in their search results, users will stop using them and start using a different search engine – their competitor.

> » **BUSINESS BLOGGING SECRETS REVEALED** «
>
> *As far as the search engines are concerned, YOU are their customer. They want to deliver a quality product to you. And their product is "relevant search results."*

By giving the search engines what they want, they rank you higher than your competitor who hasn't updated his Web site in months or perhaps years.

Blogs are new sources of quality content and because blogs are updated frequently (or should be); the search engine spiders are literally programmed to visit your blog based on how often you publish fresh content on your blog.

> **» BUSINESS BLOGGING SECRETS REVEALED «**
>
> *You can accelerate or ramp up the spider visits as you blog more frequently and on a consistent schedule.*
>
> *Think of the algorithm as the program logic that helps the spider determine how often it needs to visit your blog. You can improve your chances for good rankings by simply publishing more content, more often!*

This is why if you are using a regular Web site on its own, <u>you're at a dangerous disadvantage in the search engine ranking game</u>.

A regular Web site that's not published frequently simply cannot keep up (or catch up) with a business blog that ranks easily and quickly with top notch SEO strategies.

Once you get your content ranked high, you can market your message. You now have visibility for your target audience.

Whether your focus is toys, cars, or health food – or it's cosmetic dentistry, landscape services, or original artwork; your business blog must contain the keywords your target audience is using when they use the search engines.

Your keywords are the words and phrases that your customer or prospect has in mind when they are searching for something you have to offer.

WARNING: GEEK ALERT!

The following section is for techie readers only. Skipping this section will not reduce the SEO power of your business blog.

Continue at the next sub heading to skip the behind the curtain details revealed below.

Four Ways Blogs Act As Search Engine Magnets:

1. Blogs, by their very design, meet the current requirements for search engines and search traffic. Search engines need to deliver the latest information accurately and search engine traffic wants the most accurate information right now. Blogs are highly relevant in their niches and, at this point in time, are the best sources online for the most up-to-date information.

2. Blogs can be naturally keyword optimized for even greater appeal to search engines. By using your keywords judiciously through your blog design and blog content, you can easily rank those keywords in the search engines without gimmicks or search engine tricks. You literally begin to "rank as you write."

3. Blogs are text-rich publishing tools. What do we mean by text rich? Blogs use spider-friendly code in comparison to regular Web sites. Blogs are styled and formatted with cascading style sheets (CSS) and, for the most part, PHP with moderate use of

HTML. There are some variations in underlying code depending on the blog software you use.

The point is that blogs do not contain lots of extraneous Java or Flash coding, or poorly formatted HTML code. Blogs are designed to open the door wide to search engine spiders so that your site design doesn't get in the way of your content.

This makes your content much more visible to the search engines. The search engine spiders that visit your blog frequently can also crawl your content faster and see your content with greater clarity. This makes for easy interpretation of what your blog is talking about.

Spiders like this. Afterall, they don't want to get tangled in the web of pictures that do not give them the food they need to survive on the job.

Lots of JavaScript, flash animations and over-used HTML code hinders your content from being seen at all (JavaScript and flash) to rather difficult to interpret (too much extra code or poorly formatted pages)

4. Links are your best friend for search engines rankings. The more links you get the better. The more relevant the link, the more importance that link has for search engine results. Blogs naturally generate inbound links because in the New Media Marketplace, content links to content every moment of the day.

Great content is found by others and linked to on a regular basis. Write good content and you will get good inbound links.

Inbound links are easily generated from sites with similar content and often contain relevant keywords in the linked text to your blog. All of this means better rankings for you in the search engines with little effort spent trying to build back links and link partnerships.

Good blogging etiquette dictates that you make a practice of linking to other content when you publish – not to mention the new, amazing relationships you'll develop within the blogosphere as you link, comment, and get to know other active bloggers.

This creates outbound links and when you link to other content with relevant keywords in the linked text, it also creates a stronger relevancy rating for your blog content.

Remember to be natural and don't force the use of keywords of linked text any more than you would use your keywords throughout your blog articles.

These are just a few reasons and secrets behind why blogs are good for search engine marketing.

Blogs naturally appeal to the algorithm of search engine spiders. In other words, they have exactly what search engine spiders are programmed to look for.

In the past, producing themed site content that was rich in keywords and also had good links and navigation took more effort using a regular Web site. With blogs, all this is on autopilot and is done with the click of a button, provided you're following the plan.

FOUR KEYS TO CREATING CONTENT THAT SEARCH ENGINE SPIDERS WILL LOVE TO CRAWL

Your business blog does a lot of heavy lifting for you behind the scenes, but it will not create the content for your business blog on its own. For maximum marketing impact, you need to create content that is literal "spider bait."

You can remember the four keys to for creating search engine spider bait with the acronym FOOD:

- **F**ocus on your niche
- **O**ptimize your keywords
- **O**rganize your content
- **D**ig into your results

Focus On Your Niche

There is no replacement for researching and knowing your niche inside and out. If you've selected the right topical focus for your business blog, this will be easy. You'll already be very familiar with anything that you're passionate about or heavily involved with researching for your business.

For adding to the depth of your knowledge we recommend starting by gathering surveys and statistics on market trends happening in and around your niche.

This type of material delivers two benefits.

One is that the added research will alert you to impending shifts in your industry before your competitors.

The second is that your commentary and opinion on your research will provide tons of contextually relevant content for your business blog.

Focusing on your niche means analyzing, contributing to, or initiating the conversations taking place in your market. Remember, blogs are social tools.

There are millions of digital conversations taking place every moment as more and more people use blogs to publish and link ideas to each other.

Take Action!

Go to http://www.technorati.com and do a search for the keywords that represent and identify your niche. Go to http://www.blogdigger.com and do the same. These are blog search directories that monitor blogs in real time.

Remember to also check Google. More and more blogs are taking up top positions in Google searches, so you always want to check with Google.

Don't just check the top 10 or 20 on the first two pages. We go up to the top 40 or 50 looking specifically for blogs.

> **» BUSINESS BLOGGING SECRETS REVEALED «**
>
> *Some keywords may not have as many blogs targeting them. That's a bonus for you. Just remember to search until you have a reasonable feel for whether you will find a blog talking about something related to your niche.*
>
> *The idea is to quickly grab information from the freshest sources around for great information to share. You may also want to try http://www.topix.net and http://www.pubsub.com, but realize the information they provide is based on newsworthiness and is not necessarily niche-topic specific.*

»BUSINESS BLOGGING SECRETS REVEALED«

You need to know what conversations are taking place in your niche. You need to identify where in these conversations you can position yourself and your brand.

Search out the blogs in your niche and subscribe to them. Ask yourself the following critical questions to get the edge.

- *What are the authors saying?*

- *What comments are being posted?*

- *What gets the community excited enough to talk about in the blogosphere in your niche?*

- *What common ideas and conversations are common among all the blogs you are reading and observing?*

- *Are there any emerging trends you can identify first?*

- *Who are the top bloggers in your niche? (You will find them by the number of references to their blogs. You will start to come across these references as you explore more of the blogs in your niche.)*

This works because blogs are the fastest way to monitor the pulse of what is going on in your niche, industry or profession.

> *Blogs deliver information in real time and they represent the actual sentiment in your niches because they are free from marketing influences and mainstream media filtering.*
>
> *Blogs are the voice of consumers, and are the content creators in your niche. They tend to be authentic and authoritative sources for information.*

Optimize Your Keywords

Optimizing your keyword selection is an obvious requirement for optimizing your blog ranking. Make sure you know the right keywords to use for your niche.

With our private consulting clients and in our BLOG Interactive 360° course, we walk students through a 40-page playbook called Killer Keyword Selection that details a precise process for building an effective keyword target list right out of the gate.

Without the added education and coaching those business people have under their belt, getting too in depth here would only be confusing for the casual reader.

So, we're going to keep things simple here and give you an initial process that will jump start your keyword selection and get you going in the right direction. This way, you'll begin to carve out the right path for your business.

Applying what we're about to share with you here will give you a substantial advantage over 95% of your competitors who are currently trying to use blogs to market.

Getting Started

Go to GoodKeywords.com (and download the free software you'll find there.) This will be your tool for broad research of good keywords. Remember, your keywords are what will bring you traffic from the search engines.

To show you how Good Keywords helps with your keyword investigations, let's roll through a quick example. Let's say you have a retail store and Internet business selling lighting fixtures. On your business blog you've decided to focus your content on the niche of exterior lighting for safety and security using hidden or unique fixtures.

Using the Good Keywords tool you enter the general keyword term "lighting." Your results would look something similar to Figure 1 below.

#	Keywords	Count/Month
1	lighting	140858
2	outdoor lighting	67717
3	home lighting	15282
4	landscape lighting	14536
5	kichler lighting	11560
6	foyer lighting	10358
7	entryways fixture globe lighting used	9675
8	bathroom lighting	9224
9	progress lighting	8283
10	track lighting	8187
11	quoizel lighting	6778
12	kitchen lighting	6696
13	fluorescent lighting	6633
14	lighting chicago	6627
15	solar lighting	6403
16	recessed lighting	6272
17	cooper lighting	5088
18	lighting philadelphia	4598
19	lighting pittsburgh	4573

Figure 1

You can see that **lighting** has had 140,858 searches within the last month. That's a ton of traffic, but way too broad a term to reliably generate targeted traffic.

Looking further down the list, you see **landscape lighting** has 14,536 searches. A little further you see **copper lighting** with 5,088 searches. Just below that is **copper landscape lighting** with 2,172 searches.

What you want to consider here is which keywords represent your target audience. You may sell all types of lighting fixtures, but "landscape lighting," "copper lighting," and "copper landscape lighting" all hit your target market dead center.

Focus on using these keywords and you'll have a good start on generating top rankings and targeted traffic.

> **» BUSINESS BLOGGING SECRETS REVEALED «**
>
> *The keyword phrase with the largest amount of traffic isn't always the best for you to use.*
>
> *The more specific the keyword "phrase" you use, the better your results.*
>
> *Large amounts of traffic generally represent more general traffic for a general search term. This is usually a starting point for searches.*
>
> *Get more specific – and attract buyers!*

This is a perfect example of keywords vs. keyword phrases. These phrases represent niches that are more targeted, more specific, and more focused on what they are looking for. This is higher quality search traffic.

This is where you'll gain a major edge over your competitors. Just by knowing how to apply what you learned from your keyword research will propel you into business blogging success.

> **» BUSINESS BLOGGING SECRETS REVEALED «**
>
> *Most business owners would naturally think that the largest amount of traffic would mean the best keywords. But that's not the case.*
>
> *The fact is...*
>
> *Short Keywords = browsers*
>
> *Longer Keyword Phrases = buyers*

This is the lifeblood of targeted traffic. Searches are effective when search engines deliver results that make people happy with what they've found.

If you type "copper lighting" into Google, you want results related to "copper lighting," not results about lighting fires or spotlights. You want keywords that will make you part of those search results when someone goes searching (or shopping) for the keywords you are mentioning on your blog.

Knowing what your niche market is searching for provides you with a needs analysis of what your market wants. Keyword search tools work to help you identify where your market is.

Start with GoodKeywords.com, and when you're ready to move to a more detailed investigation, Wordtracker (www.wordtracker.com) is the research tool of choice.

> **» BUSINESS BLOGGING SECRETS REVEALED «**
>
> *Pay special attention to the two and three word "phrases." They represent more specific searches and more qualified traffic.*

It's important for higher traffic keywords to check out the number and type of sites competing on those phrases. Wordtracker and the Google Search Bar are two valuable tools for doing further research.

Wordtracker is a paid service that will provide extensive analysis and competitive research on the keywords you're considering.

The Google Search Bar is used for checking several site statistics when doing your keyword research, but the most important component is the page rank of sites showing up in current results when you're checking your potential keyword phrases.

As you investigate, write down the keywords that have the most traffic and the lowest competition. Generally speaking, these will be the ones you'll target.

We say generally here because there are times when you can target a keyword that appears to have lots of sites targeting it. That would be a situation where, when you use the Google Search Bar, you find that many sites in the top 20 results with a page rank of three or four.

We know that with the right business blog structure integrated with a solid New Media Marketing Strategy you'll quickly climb to a page rank of five or more. As you publish more content around that keyword, you'll gain ranking and rapidly begin pushing those "competitive" sites down in the rankings.

Publish content with your keywords in mind and you *will* find yourself breaking into key positions for your keywords. We've found that top-ranked pages for our keywords with page ranks four or five and less have been easily outranked by our blog content.

We've done this again and again, and every time, this proves out to be a fantastic secret strategy – for our clients as well.

As you are doing your investigation and research, write down your top choices. These keywords will eventually be your targeted keyword list. This list will eventually form the skeleton around which your blog content gets wrapped.

Organize Your Content

Now, it's time to get your blog working for you, and that means organizing your content around your keywords. We'll keep things simple here and assume you're creating a completely text-based post. (The same principles apply for audio and video Podcasts, just with a few slight twists.)

You need to specifically target these keywords as you write to inform your audience. When you have very good niche keyword phrases that also target the traffic and audience you seek, your blog will easily break into the top rankings in these areas.

This isn't as mechanical or formula-based as it may sound. The key is to know your niche instinctively and know your keywords instinctively so that writing with your keywords in mind is more natural and not as deliberate.

CHAPTER 9.5

> **» BUSINESS BLOGGING SECRETS REVEALED «**
>
> *Blog content outperforms content from standard Web sites.*
>
> *You are targeting "weak" keyword phrases because you can easily obtain good positions where pages in the search results don't have a lot of back links or very strong page rank.*

Your blogs will rank you well for your primary keyword phrases – when you work them. In the beginning, it may seem like it really is deliberate, but over time it will become natural if you take the time to understand your niche and its related search traffic.

Writing with your keywords in mind creates relevancy for your blog. The search engines will pick up your keywords and in just a short amount of time your blog content will begin to show up in the search engine results.

Blogs make ranking high in the search engines very easy. Be natural when you write your content and using your keywords because the natural language style does very well with organic (non-paid) search results.

You will begin ranking for other phrases related to your niche without even thinking about it because of this organic harmony between how you write and how search engines respond and pick up those phrases.

Dig Into Your Results

If you want to fully maximize the search engine ranking power of your business blog, it's critical that you regularly schedule time to dig into your traffic statistics.

You want to do this for two reasons.

1. To know which keywords and keyword phrases are driving traffic to your blog.

What you're looking for are keywords and phrases driving traffic to your site that you didn't specifically target.

> **» BUSINESS BLOGGING SECRETS REVEALED «**
>
> *If you see recurring instances of unsolicited or unintentional traffic and the phrases do fall within the scope of your products or services, this is a good sign that you should publish an article, a series, or a Podcast on that topic. Those phrases reveal an area of interest with your ideal audience.*

This is a sign that people are looking for information that you could use to pull more traffic to your site. Because blogs are instantly updated and blogs are indexed frequently, you can rapidly respond to this kind of traffic very quickly and drive it to your blog.

You can literally reach out and grab it! No basic Web site can do this for you and this is by no means a small thing.

We've learned more from examining how our blog is being found then we ever learned from our normal Web statistics. This is simply because of the range and reach and real time nature of blog content.

2. To discover sites that are referring traffic to you.

You must monitor your log statistics to know who is referring traffic to you. Expect this soon with a blog because blogs tend to link often to other blogs in the blogosphere.

Just like we inform you of the need to monitor your niche for market conversations, other bloggers in your niche are doing the same thing as they participate in online conversations.

> **» BUSINESS BLOGGING SECRETS REVEALED «**
>
> *Bloggers are generous promoters of great content. Always on the hunt for something good to deliver to their audience, they find information quickly and link to it without haste. They want to be the one who delivers great information first. This is part of the viral nature of blogging. Bloggers read other blogs in their areas of expertise. They cross-link to each frequently.*

This creates a rich linking infrastructure and a topically rich, focused theme-based network of sites that search engines like. For example PR (public relations) blogs tend to read other PR blogs and link to good articles and information.

> **» BUSINESS BLOGGING SECRETS REVEALED «**
>
> *This natural linking within the blogosphere creates niches of themed content that pulls search engines and traffic. If you start getting links from blogs that have good rankings and readership, your traffic can begin to grow exponentially.*

When you see these referrals, visit the blogs and see what is being said about you. It would be also be good to say "hello" and "thank you."

Participate and converse!

That's what the blogosphere is all about.

Monitoring your statistics help you understand how your blog is progressing through your niche. Are you pulling qualified traffic? Are you getting the attention of other bloggers?

If not, what can you do to attract their attention, and draw them into the conversation on your blog?

Dig into the results of your keyword focus and content creation and be prepared to act.

Ultimately, a blog alone isn't the Holy Grail for top search engine rankings.

You will need to do other things like writing high-value and relevant content for your audience.

You will need to target the keywords that your target audience is searching for, and you'll need to build links to help with your search engine popularity.

Begin with your business blog, and then kick things into overdrive by adding in other components of a complete New Media Marketing Plan.

You'll be amazed at how just a few hours per week can help you achieve results that a couple of years ago would have cost $5,000 per month or more to get!

Boosting The Performance On Your Blog

chapter ten

James T. Kirk: Evaluation, Mr. Spock.

Spock: Fascinating. That vessel is generating a force field greater than the radiation of the Earth's sun.

– *From* Star Trek *(the movie)*

》》Before moving on to ideas on how to begin expanding your New Media Marketing in section three, we'd be remiss if we didn't address ways to measure your business blogging results. As we mentioned in chapters 9 and 9.5, digging into your results is an essential part of winning with both people and search engine spiders. As with any other type of online or offline marketing, tracking is critical for success.

Far too many business owners try a marketing method, and then judge the results completely by "feel." If they didn't get many leads or any sales, they assume there must be something wrong with the marketing method.

Could it possibly be the approach simply needs to be tweaked in a few areas? Or perhaps the person applying the strategy didn't follow through on all they were supposed to?

On the other hand, "success" is assumed when leads come in and a few sales are made. With that type of thinking, the strategy or campaign is blindly repeated. No thought or analysis is given to why it's working or how the results might be improved. This is just as bad as the "poor results" scenario because very often, a lot of money is being left on the table.

Seeing these types of actions pass as research and analysis is very frustrating. This type of scattered thinking leads to a lot of lost opportunities, lost time, and, of course – lost money! I know, because I've made the same mistakes running my previous companies. It took a lot of hard lessons and persistent coaching from my mentor to pound the concept of tracking and improvement into my thick skull.

It's tough when you're dealing with the day-to-day operation of the business to take time to track, do analysis of results, and then make adjustments to try the same strategy again. But the truth is, this is how you make real money with your marketing. If you, or someone on your team, is not tracking results, improving, and trying again you're losing a lot more money than the time you think you're saving by not digging into the results.

There are really just seven simple steps to maximizing any marketing strategy, tactic or even an individual component of an ad or campaign. These principles can be applied to a broad general strategy, or to something as tightly focused as a headline.

1. Do your research on the proposed marketing strategy before using it.

2. Make sure the strategy you select aligns with your overall marketing goals and has the potential to deliver the type of results you want.

3. After deciding that it's a strategy worth pursuing, study all you can on that method.

4. If it's available – invest in working with a coach or consultant to save time and money. This puts you on the fast track to applying the strategy to your unique situation.

5. Start applying the strategy and immediately begin tracking the results.

6. Dig into the results to determine what's working, what's not, and what needs improvement.

7. Adjust or adapt one single component of the strategy and track the results again.

Repeat steps five and six until the results prove that the strategy is fully optimized.

The fact is, no marketing or for that matter any other strategy for growing your business will ever work optimally for you, if you don't fully work that method. Seems obvious, yet, this is a reason why so many businesses struggle.

Most people know they need to measure, track, and adjust, to get the best results. But for many people, knowing what to do is not the factor that's missing.

What we've discovered in working with business people and politicians around the world, is that many don't analyze results because they aren't sure what to track. And human nature indicates that when we aren't sure about something, we hesitate, procrastinate, or put it off indefinitely.

If you've fallen into this trap before, it's really not your fault. Many experts, consultants, and marketing "gurus" will, in typical mass media fashion, say you need to track your results and maximize your ROI (Return On Investment.) But general advice, and even a scientific process like the seven simple steps just listed, can have little practical meaning if you don't know exactly what to measure and how to track it.

Why Measuring A Blog's Effectiveness Is Different Than The Typical Web site

Tracking, measuring, and improving upon the performance of your business blog, is different than a static Web site and more typical Web Marketing 1.0 methods. Just as we discussed in chapter five, some things carry over to Web Marketing 2.0. But New Media Marketing is a different animal, and it needs a different type of tracking.

Here's why. Except for the up-front cost of the self-hosted blog installation, and the very low cost of your hosting or a monthly subscription to a third-party blog-software hosting service – the hard costs of connecting with your target audience is near zero.

When you write an article for your blog, that doesn't cost you a dime in production costs. You or someone on your team is spending time, and in business – time is money. That's true, but don't let this type of thinking mislead you.

Time is being spent every day on all types of business activities. It's not a question of whether time needs to be dedicated or not. The question is what's the ROI on that time.

In chapter seven, we covered in detail how to determine your budget for marketing with blogs and New Media by using the Lifetime Value of your customers. Now may be a good time to go back and reread the tail end of that chapter to remind yourself how to properly frame your view of time dedicated to these actions.

The fact is marketing with New Media has extremely low production costs. Even audio and video Podcasts syndicated through your business blog have extremely low production costs. Time commitments may seem more significant; yet when compared with other marketing strategies, they're the same or less. Plus, marketing with blogs and other New Media has exponential results that don't necessarily all come at the front end of an event.

For example, you can publish one article that can reach hundreds, thousands, and hundreds of thousands of people right out of the gate. Then, via the search engines and RSS, that article continues to drive traffic, open a dialogue, and build relationships with an ongoing stream of prospects far into the future. All this happens with the time invested in one article or post.

Unlike a traditional direct-marketing campaign, you don't have the same costs of acquisition associated with reaching a target audience with your message.

How To Measure Your Blog Return on Investment (ROI)

So how do you measure results, when you can publish content that thousands of people can see now, and for decades to come? How can you measure ROI, if there is no direct cost associated with each person who sees that content?

You're not as limited as you might think. It requires a shift in your thinking to the New Media Marketing Mindset, like we talked about in chapter five. It requires new areas of tracking and measurement to expand on what's typically tracked in Web Marketing 1.0.

Here are five important areas to track and measure for adaptation and improvement with your business blog. As you expand your New Media Marketing beyond business blogging, other metrics will be required.

The following will give you a rock-solid foundation in maximizing the effectiveness of your efforts right from the start.

1. Traffic

Traffic is one of the first ways to measure the success of your blog. It's important to be patient and work your business blogging strategy. Traffic will come, if you leverage and tweak the natural promotional properties of your blog. We are not talking tricks. We're talking about using your blog strategically for maximum results.

Initially, using the traffic statistics program included in your Web hosting package will be sufficient. For many businesses – that will be all you need. Most hosting companies include this free as part of your package. You can find it by logging into your Web hosting control panel and looking for an icon or link that says "stats."

If you're using a third-party blog hosting option, like TypePad.com, then we recommend using a separate site-measuring tool to help you build a better picture of your blog traffic. Site Meter (www.sitemeter.com) is a popular option. Blog Patrol is another (www.blogpatrol.com).

What To Look For

Here are some questions you'll want to ask yourself as you review your traffic statistics. Use this as a starting point. Then create your own unique set of specific questions to reflect your specific goals and business blogging strategy.

- What are you visitor numbers and page views?

    Are the numbers of your visitors steadily growing? Are you seeing an increase in page views rising as a regular trend?

- Were there any spikes in traffic during a particular period during the month? If so, what went on that day or around that time?

    It's important to know if a particular article, Podcast, or special event generated that traffic. Maybe it was another blogger, news source, or other outside referrer that generated that traffic.

    For instance, we see our traffic spike every week when our regular business columns come out in the newspapers. We're able to isolate and track the impact of that one article as a result of traffic spike we see in our statistics.

    You always want to know where your traffic spikes are coming from, because it lets you know what's working, so you can repeat that activity over and over again.

- How are you doing in comparison to last month? How are you doing compared to last year at the same time?

- What pages are popular on your site?

    What links get the most clicks? If you're promoting your blog from the main page of your Web site, take a look at your traffic and see how many people are clicking through to your blog.

    Do you see interest growing, and are people returning to your blog? Repeat visits are a good indication of your "stickiness," and that is important as an indicator on the quality of your content.

- How are people finding you through search engines? What search terms are they using? The stats program will give you insight into that.

- How many RSS requests are you getting?

    Another way to measure stickiness is by looking at the percentage of repeat visitors vs. the number of new RSS subscriptions you have. Don't rely too heavily on this metric though, unless the bulk of your target audience is "techies."

    If your audience is primarily made up of techies already comfortable with RSS, and you're using a self-hosted blog like WordPress, you'll want to use an RSS subscription tracking tool like Feed Burner (www.feedburner.com) to measure activity.

    Feed Burner provides excellent processing of your RSS feed by providing features such as: subscriber metrics, RSS advertising, feed conversion, Podcasting, and much more.

    If you're using a third-party blog, the hosts usually provide some basic statistics. Blog Harbor is one of the better ones that provides you with several stat metrics you can use to measure your RSS reads and blogs visits.

No matter what, you must have a way to measure your traffic and see what your results are so you know what you need to improve, change, or remove with your business blogging strategy.

2. Search Engines

Unlike a regular Web site, you can measure your blog progress in a matter of hours, and respond appropriately in real time. We've found this to be invaluable when using business blogging to boost search engine rankings.

For example, on one of our blogs we had an important keyword, which we were intensely going after top rankings for. Because of the site's membership structure, it was getting no keyword ranking higher than 100. Solely using our business blog, we had gotten to the point where we were ranking in the top 20 – around 12 and 13 – and we kept jumping up back and forth to eight or nine.

So we played with that blog title, arranged the keywords for the best combination that Google would like, changed some key areas of blog posts – and bingo! We found the right combo, and now we are consistently ranking between #1 to #3 against a top international competitor with 500 franchises who's spending thousands each month to battle us with Web Marketing 1.0 strategies.

Needless to say, we're quite happy. ☺ Especially considering we didn't spend a dime to get there.

This is an example of how powerful blogs can be targeting a top keyword.

Another even more impressive way to use your business blog to drive traffic is to use what's called an "edge-traffic keyword." This is a keyword that doesn't get a whole lot of searches, but that highly qualifies your audience – people who will be extremely open to other topics on our blog. These types of keywords bring us a nice bit of traffic to our blog.

As you can probably tell by now – measuring your blog ROI for search engines is done by examining your search engine rankings. You will rank for lots of keywords naturally and bring traffic from unexpected sources. A continuous focus on a core set of strategically targeted keywords will ultimately determine the ranking success of your business blog.

A quick way to measure your blog's success for search engine traffic with Google is to go to http://www.googlerankings.com and type in your blog URL and a keyword or keyword phrase. Googlerankings.com will tell you if and where you rank in the top 1,000.

Here's an even better way to do it:

> **» BUSINESS BLOGGING SECRETS REVEALED «**
>
> *Go to http://www.nichebot.com/ranking/ and type in a list of* **all** *your keywords to check your blog URL against all of your keyword terms. If you still don't know where you rank, then make sure you change the last drop-down box from Top 100 to Top 1000 to make sure you check all the rankings.*

3. Comments

Comments are a great way to measure how compelling your blog content is becoming for your audience. This is a bit tricky though, because blog traffic takes some time to warm up; so you will need to promote and encourage interaction and solicit reader responses. Business blogs will always take longer and have more of a challenge getting people to engage in commenting.

Don't be discouraged with this at first.

- Stick with it.
- Give it time.

- Work on writing great content that is compelling for your readers and keeps them informed.
- Stay passionate and committed to your topic.

Slowly but surely, you will see people start to leave comments at different posts throughout your blog. We make it a practice of responding to all comments as soon as we can even if the visitor doesn't return.

> **» BUSINESS BLOGGING SECRETS REVEALED «**
>
> *Replying to all comments left on your blog demonstrates to others coming through that you are involved and participating with your audience. It makes you approachable and gives you one more measurable success metric.*

4. Word Of Mouth (inbound links)

Links to your business blog are one way to measure buzz and word-of-mouth marketing. They carry a lot of weight because links from blogs carry a message that influences others. Links to your blog are a way to measure the amount of viral activity that is occurring with your blog.

You can go to a service like http://www.technorati.com and do a search on your blog URL.

Technorati will return a list to you of all the links to your blog from other blogs. Technorati.com monitors all the blogs and links among blogs in real time. It's a great way to track the word-of-mouth index for your blog.

A tool for measuring a broader source of links is URL Trends (www.urltrends.com). It's much more than just inbound links that URL Trends monitors, so it's something worth checking out. They have membership levels from free to big-ticket plans with varying levels of data mining.

Either way, some of the questions you want to answer are:

- Who is linking to you?
- How influential are these blogs?
- What are others saying about you?
- How many links are incoming?
- Are the blogs linking to you representative of your core audience?
- How much traffic is being driven through these back links?

Quality is what matters here. Lots of links are good, but you want links that say something good about you. Just as with comments, be patient. Give your content time to circulate and be found by others who will want to link to it.

TrackBacks are also a good measure of buzz and word-of-mouth marketing. Pay attention to your TrackBack links and visit the blogs referencing you to see what they are saying. The quality of your TrackBack links will grow as you continue to produce good content.

Remember – write good content that connects, educates, and impacts your target audience.

5. Narrow Target Tracking

Along with all the more general aspects of your business blog, you also want very specific metrics like leads, newsletter subscriptions, and sales. But to do that, you must be able to measure those results independently.

For example, to track leads, you need a separate software program that allows you to assign a special tracking code to a text link or display ad. That code will allow you to track whether people take the action you want them to when they get to whatever landing you're sending them to.

With sales, you can use tracking codes for measuring click-throughs from a specific location. This is extremely helpful for tracking how people go to your sales page from your blog, or even from individual posts on your blog. With some programs, you'll even be able to compare the number of click-throughs to the number of people who buy.

If you have a newsletter, your success can be measured by comparing traffic verses the number of subscribers you get via your blog.

Here are three top software recommendations to consider when doing your narrow tracking. All are very good programs, but we've listed them starting with the easiest to manage to more in-depth data mining.

Adtrackz www.MyAdTrackz.com

Dynatracker www.1DynaTracker.com

3D Stats www.3dstats.com

Your Content

Monitoring the performance of your content involves tracking which articles get the most attention or clicks. In other words, you want to determine which articles are the most popular with your traffic and subscribers.

With WordPress you can add a simple plug-in (free add-in module) that helps you monitor the popularity of posts right from your blog admin panel. Blog Harbor has specific stats for determining your most popular articles. Feed Burner also provides statistics on which articles are popular with your RSS subscribers.

If your blog is on another third-party hosted blog, you can use Stat Counter to determine why articles are getting the most traffic according to keywords. Keeping tabs on how your content is performing for your readers and the search engines is an important part of shaping an effective and useful business blog.

By measuring your blog performance by tracking narrow target results, you'll begin to build a clear picture of how well your blog is doing, and how each and every adjustment, tweak, or addition impacts performance and ROI.

With consistent monitoring and some fine-tuning, you'll quickly turn your business blog into the fully optimized core of a more complete New Media Marketing Strategy.

Section III

≫Influence & Persuasion Secrets Revealed!

Tribal Marketing, The Secret Source Of High Leverage Influence With Your Target Audience

chapter eleven

"Perhaps it is good to have a beautiful mind, but an even greater gift is to discover a beautiful heart."

– John Nash, "A Beautiful Mind"
Nobel Prize winner on Game Theory

>>> It was a sunny mid-April afternoon in 1992 when the call I'd been waiting for came in. I didn't realize it at the time, but the gentleman on the other end of the line would become the direct gateway to a niche audience that would award us with more than $11 million over the next five years.

At the time, I was running a landscape design and construction company which I started my senior year in college. The call came from one of the dozen neighborhoods we had been targeting in the tri-county area.

This particular neighborhood was a development of brand-new, high-end residences just outside of Princeton, NJ with a high concentration of homes owned by business owners.

The conversation started out innocently enough with Larry explaining that he was dissatisfied with the architect and contractor currently working on his project. We met the next week, hit it off, and the job ended up being our first project over a quarter million dollars.

Larry was an influencer within the tribe of successful business owners. He owned a very profitable investment company who handled investments for wealthy individual investors and small countries around the world.

Over the following months, he and I became friends as we talked about everything from politics and relationships to entrepreneurship and high performance cars.

When Larry's friends and neighbors would stop by, I'd always get a personal introduction. Since most of his friends and neighbors were business owners as well, my relationships grew rapidly with a new niche audience before his project was even finished. Not to mention, I really enjoyed my work because I really enjoyed talking with the people we served.

Over the next five years, that one relationship with Larry would lead directly to millions more in revenue. More importantly, it opened the door to a group of wealthy business owners that would often have our project schedule booked over a year in advance.

What happened with Larry? Was this just a case of referral-based marketing? Or was it something more?

Referral Marketing is a very powerful strategy. And sure, referrals played a role in our gaining favor with this audience of successful business owners. But there was something more.

I didn't just get those personal introductions because of the superior work my team was doing. I had been positioned as an expert and the best in my industry because Larry and I had trust, rapport, and respect for one another.

I didn't realize it at the time, but I had blindly stumbled into the effective application of Tribal Marketing.

This is a powerful strategy for marketing not only to the affluent – but also to any niche, group, or target audience you can imagine. It is an extremely effective marketing strategy built on relationships, rapport, and communication. And it works equally well both offline and online.

The Tribal Marketing Construct

All successful marketers understand the importance of knowing their target audience. We've made the case throughout this book for knowing your target audience in order to successfully market with New Media.

But what's the most effective way to get the word out to your target audience?

How do you achieve a trusted and respected position with that audience?

The fastest, most reliable, and least costly method is by employing the Tribal Marketing Strategy.

When we say "Tribal" here, we're not simply suggesting you think of your target audience as one single group called a "Tribe."

That's a step in the right direction, since the word implies a societal or cultural construct. But it doesn't give you a complete picture of influential hierarchies, and without that, you can't plan a practical approach to leverage significant influence and persuasion within that niche.

Without understanding the entire Tribal construct, you're likely to waste a lot of time, money, and effort trying to win over your target audience.

CHAPTER ELEVEN

Tribal Marketing does not equate your target audience with a single group called a "Tribe" because a Tribe is made up of sub-groups. Tribal Marketing actually breaks down the target audience into four distinct sub-groups, which makes it much easier to successfully plan your positioning with the audience.

The following diagram (figure 11-1) shows how these four groups are put together and relate to each other.

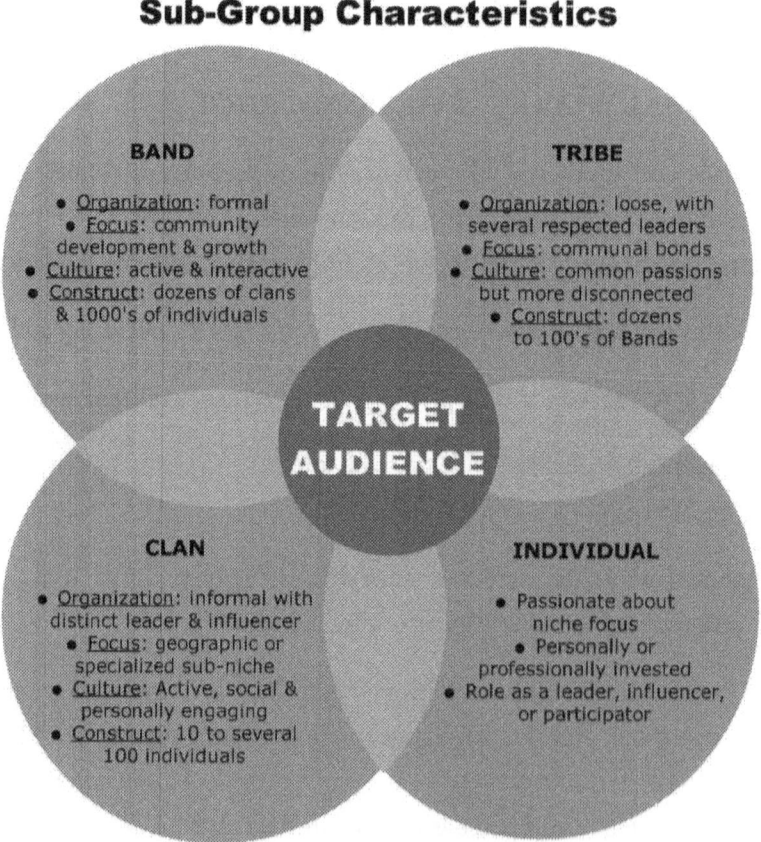

IMAGE figure 11-1

Tribal Marketing is based on historical structures of society. And just like those past cultures, you see that a target audience in the Tribal Marketing construct is made up of Individuals, Clans, and Bands which together ultimately form "The Tribe."

The Tribal level holds a tremendous amount of influential power when you're positioned properly in front of the entire Tribe, but that positioning isn't easily gained. Figure 11-2 shows you why.

Tribal Marketing Power Matrix

	Social Connection	
Influence Impact	**Strong**	**Weak**
High	BAND	TRIBE
Low	CLAN	INDIVIDUAL

IMAGE figure 11-2

Chapter Eleven

The Tribe is the largest group of all four. It has the weakest social structure. This makes it a more challenging target for leveraging influence and persuasion.

Thanks to their tightly knit structure, integrated organization, and greater interactivity, the Tribal Clans and Bands are where leverage is the easiest to achieve.

This really isn't difficult to see in real life. Take for example, the Tribe of motorcycle riders, and in particular the target audience of people who ride sport bikes.

Back in 1989, I bought my first sport bike. I immediately fell in love with the speed, handling, and freedom of that machine. I was passionate about motorcycle riding, but other than a few friends from town, I didn't really know anyone I could ride with on a regular schedule.

Then one day as I was leaving Gold's Gym with my helmet in hand, a guy stopped me and asked if that was my bike parked outside. My answer "Yes" led to a 45-minute conversation and invitation to ride with him and a group of other sport bike riders that weekend.

That weekend was my first introduction to a Tribal Clan in the Tribal Marketing construct. It was a group of about two dozen riders who regularly came together from all over northern New Jersey to meet with two things in common – a passion for sport bikes and speed.

Luckily, that first Tribal Clan I joined had seven state police troopers, including the guy who invited me to join them. ☺

Eventually, with a new bike, and a desire to ride on more challenging roads, several other guys from that group and I crossed over to a new Tribal Clan.

This new group was a little bit larger, and had a much more distinct leadership hierarchy. There was a weekly meeting of the group at 7a.m. every Sunday, weather permitting.

The most respected man in this new Tribal Clan was Bill.

Bill also happened to be on the board of a large sport bike association. With a legal, nonprofit structure and nearly 10,000 members, this association would definitely be considered a Tribal Band in the Tribal Marketing construct.

At Bill's suggestion, I joined the sport bike association, as well. Now, I was a member of both a Tribal Clan and a Tribal Band, and all the while, I was part of the broader Tribe of "sport bike riders."

What does all this have to do with your marketing? I'll explain.

When I was riding and racing regularly, I devoured every type of magazine and book I could on sport bikes and racing strategies. I even paid attention to hundreds of advertisements and watched plenty of commercials during televised races (Tribe level target marketing.)

When it came time to buy equipment for my bike, I went to the suppliers who sponsored the sport bike association (the Tribal Band level.) My trust and comfort was there.

Sponsors came in all types and sizes. To get a top sponsorship spot cost big bucks. But surprisingly, the fastest way to a coveted prime sponsorship spot was not always with the most money.

For instance, I remember this new company that had excellent products, but not a lot of capital behind them. The owner of this company started riding with us on Sundays, which made him a member of our Tribal Clan.

Yet even with this "membership," if he approached the sport bike association directly with the marketing budget he had, he would've been lucky to get some low-level sponsorship positioning at a few race events – at best.

But this savvy business owner didn't go that route. He used the relational power of Tribal Marketing to get top sponsorship positioning – without spending any extra money.

The owner of this new company built a relationship with Bill, the "unofficial" leader of our Tribal Clan.

Bill, being a respected member of the board for the sport bike association, recommended this brand-new company to be a top sponsor for that year's race events. Even with an already over-booked sponsorship roster, premium sponsorship placement was "magically" created.

That's Tribal Marketing in action!

The Tribal Marketing Advantage

Fortunately for you, most business professionals don't understand how to effectively market to a target audience this way.

The Tribal level is where most experienced sales professionals and marketers put their full attention, because they see their target audience as one big Tribe.

As a result, they're leaving you a wide-open opportunity to seize untapped and unrecognized sub-groups, all for yourself! And with that, also giving you the opportunity to climb an internal 'Influence Ladder' (more on that in a few seconds) right to the top of the entire Tribe.

The matrix in figure 11-3 shows how most business owners and marketers approach their target audience.

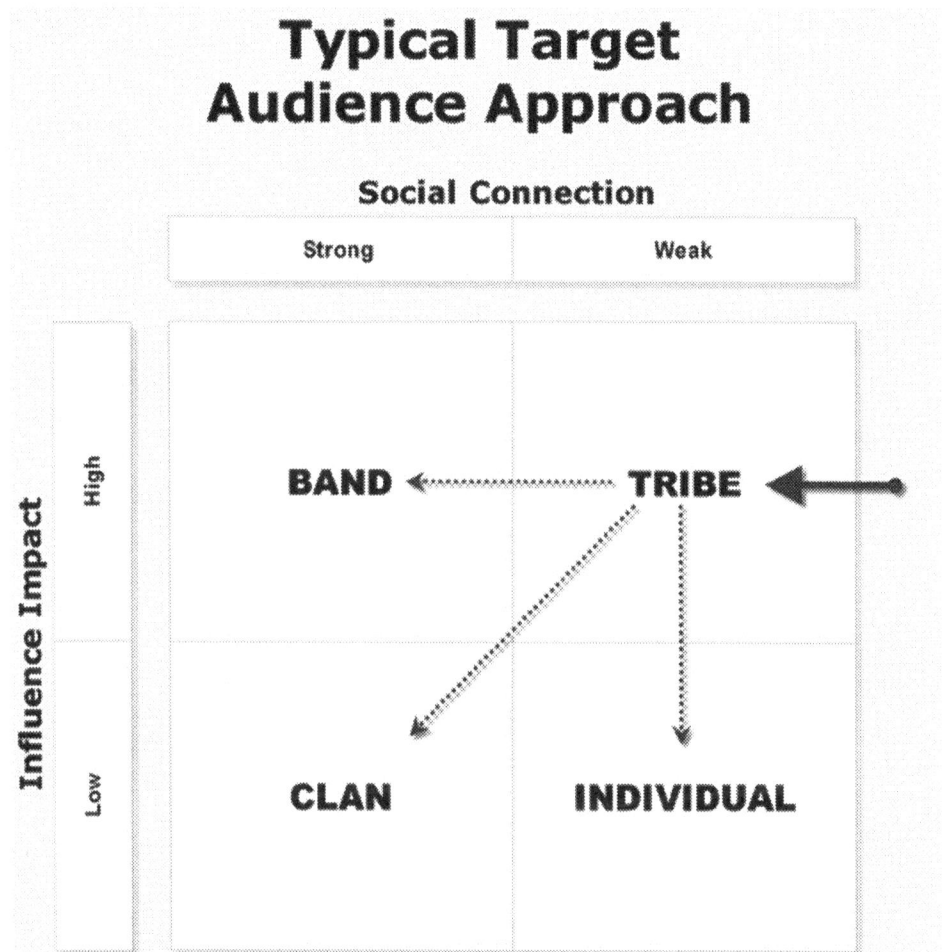

Figure 11-3

With the goal of connecting with qualified prospects, the typical target audience approach is tackled from the top down. The business owner or marketer goes straight for top positioning in front of the entire Tribe.

This method has serious flaws in it; mainly, because there are only two ways to market with this type of top-down approach to a target audience.

1. A mass marketing style campaign "speaking" at the target audience
OR

2. A connection and relationship with a highly popular Tribe level leader

Don't get us wrong. Influence, recognition, and reputation with the entire Tribe are the ultimate goal for most business owners and marketers.

Any time you can go straight to the top of the Tribe and influence from the top down, that's awesome – more power to you!

You can always get lucky and hook up with one of the "top dogs" right out of the gate, and we applaud our clients when this happens.

Most people need a strategic approach in order to get to the top. (Think about Oprah, and how many levels you need to climb in order to pitch your book, product, or idea to get on her show.)

So unless you think you can speak directly to Oprah, (perhaps you go to the same spa, or live in her neighborhood on the island of Maui) consider the following new approach to get to the influence leaders you need access to in your niche, industry, or target audience.

It Can't Be Bought

Remember, you can't buy your way into the Tribal Influence level. It's extremely difficult to connect with a Tribal level influencer or leader without a personal recommendation or established credibility from within the Tribe.

You can still allocate some of your resources and attention in this direction. But at the same time, invest your primary focus and energy toward creating relationships in the Tribal sub-groups.

The more efficient and reliable way to gain influence with an entire Tribe is by becoming known at the Tribal Clan and Band levels. The fastest way to a respectable position at those levels is through relationships with individuals.

But – not just any individual.

Your goal is to look for individuals who are influencers – individuals who will champion your cause, and give you important personal introductions. Individuals like Larry, the deca-millionaire, or Bill from my motorcycle racing days.

Figure 11-4 shows what this looks like.

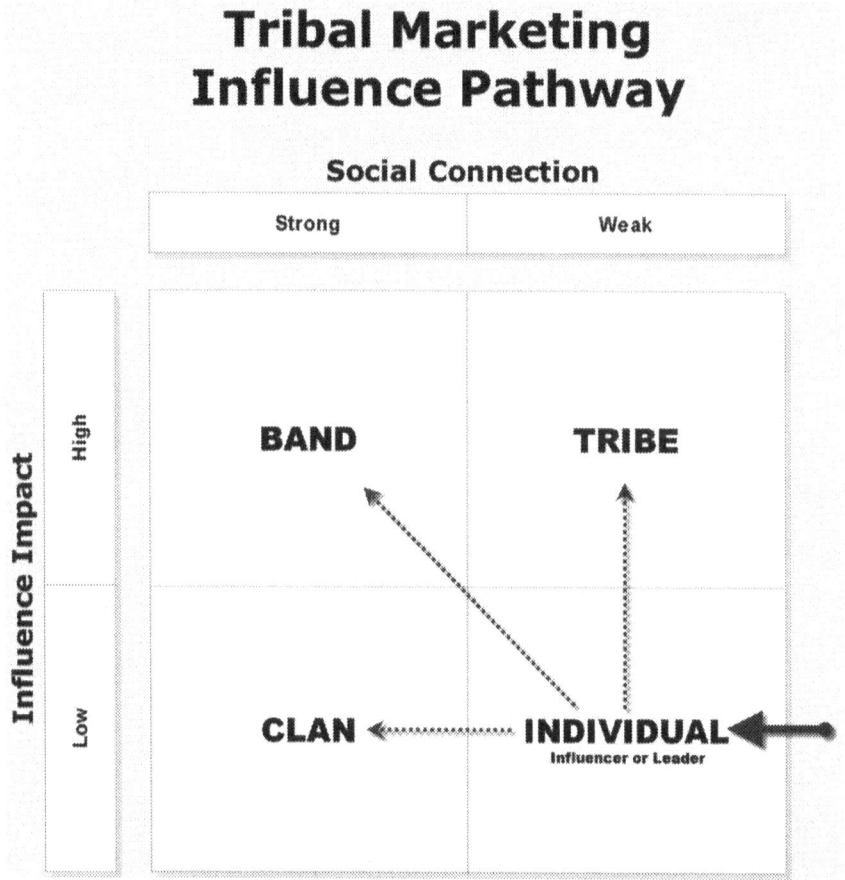

Figure 11-4

When your goal is to influence the influencers, instead of trying to "sell" or market to the entire Tribe – you'll gain more credibility and respect within the Tribe as a whole. Sometimes you'll have so much business coming from your involvement with a single Tribal Band, like I had with Larry, that you may not even need recognition by the entire Tribe.

Marketing to the Affluent by Dr. Thomas J. Stanley is one book that's required reading for members in our Business Owner's Coaching Club.

If you're going to position yourself as <u>the</u> expert when using the Tribal Marketing Strategy, Dr. Stanley's three books on Marketing, Selling and Networking to the Affluent are great resources. Reading them together will immediately give you great ideas on high result selling styles that align with your personality, interests, and strengths.

We got hooked on his book series with *The New York Times* bestseller, *The Millionaire Next Door*. His writing style is so full of practical case studies and examples that you'll devour his books in one sitting, and come back to them again and again as "reference manuals" for your business.

THE INFLUENCE LADDER IS THE KEY TO HIGH-LEVERAGE TRIBAL MARKETING

Sometimes the Tribe you're trying to gain positioning with is large, geographically diverse, and without a formal structure.

In this case, you can still apply the methodology of Tribal Marketing with what's called an Influence Ladder.

Let's say you're the owner of Black Box Security, a Chicago-based security company. Your top-selling product comes with superior service, providing 24/7 protection including personal security and safety for people, no matter where they are in the world.

Your target audience is comprised of wealthy individuals, many of whom are affluent owners of luxury real estate. You know that magazine advertisements or introduction packages, no matter how impressive they are, will NOT get you the results you need to successfully position yourself with this Tribe.

So, you begin brainstorming... *Who is a top influencer with affluent owners of exclusive real estate?*

Who is someone that the majority of the people in this scattered Tribe would respect the opinion of?

Donald Trump comes to mind.

He'd probably be an excellent source of influence with that Tribe, right?

But you don't know anyone of influence who knows him. So what's your apparent choice? Walk into "The Donald's" New York City office, try to get past his gatekeeper, and get an immediate appointment?

You're clouded with grandiose thinking, so you continue with positive affirmations, to picture this scenario taking place.

With your best Brooklyn accent, you extend your right hand, and walk straight up to Donald Trump with sheer confidence.

"Yo, Don, how you doin'?"

Ok, so that's a little bit of an exaggeration with the outer-borough accent, but seriously – even if you were polished in your approach – how far do you think you'd get with that? Sure, everyone gets lucky, once in a while, but seriously, how lucky would you have to be with this approach?

Instead, what if you took a look at the Influence Ladder leading to Mr. Trump?

Being from Chicago, you realize that you have a friend who is buddies with a longtime friend of Bill Rancic.

Yes, the same Bill Rancic who won the coveted job with Donald Trump on *The Apprentice* TV show that first aired on NBC in the Spring of 2004, and has been one of the most successful, and prominent hires from the show.

After two years of top performance, Bill has won Trump's favor and trust; so you know an introduction from Bill would get you at least a few minutes of face-time with The Donald.

You also know that this longtime friend of Bill's is a fantastic person, and based on what your friend has shared, you both have a lot in common. So you get introduced to Bill's friend, you hit it off, and the relationship grows with time.

Now, before we go any further with this scenario, it's critical that you're not just using Bill's friend. You'd have to truly enjoy spending time with this person in order for a real friendship to develop – helping him out in any way you could, and honestly caring about his success, like you would with any other friend.

The way to tell if you're "using" someone is to ask yourself; *"If everything was to fall apart with the Influence Ladder, would I still remain friends with this person?"*

If you can honestly answer yes, then you're on solid moral ground.

Back to Rancic and Trump...

Eventually you get introduced to Mr. Rancic. Once again, you don't see Bill as a rung on the Influence Ladder. You see him as a friend – a pretty cool friend, at that! He's extremely bright, and your conversations are always stimulating to the point where you generate new ideas every time you get together.

It just so happens that with your connections with several specialty importers of marble, you're able to help Bill smooth out some bumps in his management on the construction of The Trump International Hotel and Tower in Chicago.

Do you think Bill is now going to feel deeply grateful, perhaps even indebted to you? So do you think he'll be eager to set up an introduction with Mr. Trump when you ask?

Of course!

After all, you've proven yourself to be a helpful contributor to his goals and success. Now he feels that his introduction would be a valuable one that his boss would also benefit from, and he'll look great just for knowing someone like you, and fostering the introduction.

Now with a personal introduction to Donald Trump – along with a brilliant pitch you've prepared – you're in!

That's how the Influence Ladder and Tribal Marketing work hand-in-hand.

The New Media Marketplace Takes Tribal Marketing Online

Up until the last few years, Tribal Marketing has been primarily an offline strategy. The first decade of Internet development with the mass media mindset did little to foster culture that was healthy for Tribal Marketing online.

It would appear at first glance, with rapid Internet and technology development that individualism is on the rise. While that may be true in some cases, the rise of the New Media Marketplace has already reversed this trend.

Every month, millions of new people are joining memberships to participate in online social networks. The individualism and isolation that many felt with the Internet in the nineties is quickly eroding.

As you saw in the first three chapters of this book, the New Media Marketplace is radically different than mass media and the initial online environment molded by mass marketing.

Interruption marketing is dying a slow, ugly death. You need to connect, communicate, and converse with your target audience. That target audience cannot be approached with the mass marketing mindset.

All this positions Tribal Marketing not just as an option for effectively connecting with your target audience online. It's the only effective strategy, if you want results without breaking the bank.

But the impact is not just effective with exclusively offline or exclusively online Tribes.

The New Media Marketplace now makes this easier than ever before to create a click-and-mortar crossover. *(Click-and-mortar = Combining a Brick and Mortar Business with the Internet using online strategies in conjunction with offline strategies.)*

New Media makes it possible to leverage Tribal Marketing online and offline synergistically.

Previous to the New Media Marketplace, various sub-groups would have their primary interaction offline. Now, people are looking for products and services that not only deliver solutions, but also link them to others – to a community, to a Tribe.

People are looking for products and services that not only solve problems, but also connect them to others with similar interests.

All this is very exciting when you understand Tribal Marketing, and it should be, because it works <u>with</u> the changing marketplace. It makes you a partner with consumers, not a marketing antagonist.

The even better news is that making these Tribal Marketing connections is easier than you might think when you know how to work with the New Media Marketplace.

Now, let's take a look at how you influence the influencers.

Influencing The Influencers... The Keys To Winning With Personal Persuasion!

chapter twelve

"The Game of Chess is not merely an idle amusement. Several very valuable qualities of the mind useful in life are acquired and strengthened by it, so much so they become habits ready when needed.

For life is a kind of Chess Game. We often have points to gain, and competitors or adversaries to contend with. There are a vast variety of good and bad events that are in some degree the effect of careful thought, or the want of it.

By playing at Chess then, we may learn: 1st, Foresight, which looks a little into the future, and considers the consequences that may result from an action ... 2nd, Circumspection, which surveys the whole Chess-board, or scene of

Chapter Twelve

> *action – the relation of several pieces, and their situations;*
> *... 3rd, Caution, not to make our moves too hastily..."*
>
> – *Benjamin Franklin*

》The ability to influence and persuade – do you have it?

It's what all business owners and politicians want, whether they admit it publicly or not. That's because influence and persuasion, when creatively combined with the right strategies, will lead to more customers, profits, or votes.

The power of influence and persuasion is not something we're born with. We live our infant and toddler lives crying for what we want and stomping our feet when we don't get it. Hardly, what could be considered influencing behaviors.

It's only as children and young teens that we begin to see how the world really works. By that time, our environment and upbringing have already been intertwined with our personalities.

From that point forward, it becomes difficult to tell where the "natural" behavior ends and "learned" behavior begins without outside help.

Sure, some people appear to be "born naturals." They may have some apparent advantages, but the fact is that most people who have learned and practiced the right strategies, (either intentionally or by happenstance) surpass most of those "gifted" individuals who took their gifts for granted.

Ronald Reagan left his legacy in history, known as the Great Communicator. The fall of the Berlin wall and the collapse of the Soviet Union were accomplished as much by influence in a single, personal relationship with Mikhail Gorbachev, as they were by political and economic pressures.

Yet as a child, Reagan was a loner who had a hard time making friends.

Oprah Winfrey's foundation for influential greatness in her adulthood began with a childhood of abuse and poverty. She could have turned all that inward with self-destructive behavior.

Instead, Oprah transformed her environment into a multi-billion dollar media empire, because she harnessed the power to influence the masses.

Paul Orfalea started Kinko's and grew it into a $1.5 billion a year company that *Fortune* named one of the best places in America to work. Much of his success is due to his stellar connection and rapport building skills, but it was dyslexia that was the root of that success.

The success stories of these and thousands of others all have one thing in common. Each took what the world would consider weakness and turned it into success and riches through the art of influence.

It took strength, persistence, and practice – but it got done!

You can do the same.

Whether you consider yourself a "natural" influencer or not, it doesn't matter. You simply need to understand that all it takes is the right set of strategies and some practice.

Offline Vs. Online

It's pretty easy to see influence and persuasion at work in the offline world.

You meet a person and immediately begin building or breaking rapport with your first face-to-face meeting. Offline you can pick up visual cues like body language, tone of voice, or rate of speech. You have all five senses working for you, which would seem to make the goal of gaining influence easier.

Online influence and persuasion seems like it would be a more difficult task.

And that would be true… if we were talking about the online world in terms of Web Marketing 1.0. That was an online environment where conversations were limited, and what passed for "engaging" was a 40-page sales letter, an animated Flash ad, or some stale corporate Web site.

With the New Media Marketplace powered by people, participation, and conversation, there's a more "natural" form of persuasion that comes into play.

It's much easier to find your target audience gathered together in Tribal Clans, Bands, or as the entire Tribe itself. Audio and video along with the instant interaction and ongoing conversations created by blogs, Podcasts and social networks make online persuasion with those groups even easier than traditional offline meetings.

As you saw in the last chapter, your goal is not just to influence the masses within your target audience. It's equally, if not more important, to "influence the influencers" using the Tribal Marketing strategies we introduced. That means building rapport, relationships, and trust with influencers on a one-on-one basis.

Clearly, the savvy businessperson who has mastered their soft-skills, will have the edge when influencing the influencers both offline and online.

Achieving online persuasion can be easier than offline meetings because all the clues to a person's style are right there in front of your eyes – if you know what to look for, and where to find it.

Face-to-face influence requires top-notch people reading skills, along with near instant adaptation and response skills. When meeting people online, you have time to do research on a person before ever conversing with them for the first time.

Not just "surface" research like: who they are, what interests they have, or their professional background. We're talking about insight into their communication and motivation style.

This is the insight that can make the difference between building or breaking rapport, right from the start.

Before we get carried away and start talking about all the cool ways to read people online and build powerful win-win relationships with Tribal Influencers – there's someone more important for you to influence first.

Influence And Persuasion Starts With You

Ask anyone what first comes to mind when you say the word "influence" or "persuasion," and see what they say. Chances are nine out of ten people will give you an answer that has to do with "other people."

After all, isn't that the idea – to win friends and influence people?

You bet! That's the ultimate end goal.

Yet, we can tell you from our experience working with hundreds of business owners and politicians around the world, along with countless public case studies, that influence and persuasion starts with YOU first and foremost!

Think about it.

If you can't influence or motivate yourself to take action, how can you ever effectively motivate anyone else around you?

The fact is – you won't.

At least not as effectively and effortlessly as you would, if you had a good understanding of what makes people "tick" differently – starting with yourself.

To maximize your influence and persuasion in your marketing, sales, management, or any area of life – offline or online – it all starts with you. The first place to start is with your own Natural Style.

You're A Natural!

We each have our own unique way of communicating, connecting, and getting things done. It's called your "Natural Communication Style."

Your Natural Style determines:

- How you interact with the outside world
- How others perceive you
- How you talk to yourself
  (Yes, everybody does it. Just not everybody admits it. ☺)

The better you understand yourself, the faster you'll reach your goals. In fact – <u>what you don't know about yourself, keeps you from getting what you want in business and in life</u>.

The good news is that you can quickly figure out what your Natural Style is and how you need to adapt.

It's like breaking a complex code to a hidden treasure that contains all the riches you'll ever need. Learning your own Natural Style is the beginning to breaking your own code.

Knowing your own code gives you the ability to quickly adapt, and adaptation gives you control.

- Control over how you manage and motivate yourself
- Control over how other people perceive you
- Control over how you adapt to others and build rapport
- Control over how quickly you can persuade and influence others

Over the last three years in working with hundreds of business owners, sales professionals, and politicians, we've developed a simple, scientific system called The Influence Code™ that maximizes your influence and persuasion.

In this system, there are four dimensions that give you complete control over your personal performance and ability to reach your biggest goals.

These four dimensions of influence are – Communication, Motivation, Focus, and Mindset.

In the complete Influence Code™ system, all four dimensions include a series of scientifically validated assessments that make the detailed discovery of your Natural Style in each dimension fast, precise, and fun. You then get a complete personal code for each dimension that equips you to adapt, connect, and get the results you want in all areas of business and life – all with fewer mistakes and in less time.

While it takes a full seven days seminar to immerse people in all four dimensions at once, we're going to share an introduction to the first dimension (Communication) right now.

The Communication Code™ deals with your natural communication and behavioral styles. It's all about how you take action and get things done, including how you communicate and connect (or don't connect) with other people.

What you're about to learn here with this introduction alone, will put you light years ahead of your competitors.

Let's get started with the four-step process that will put you on the path to persuasion mastery.

The Four Stages of Persuasion Mastery

Persuasion doesn't just pop out of a box nice and neat, all complete and put together. You can't buy it, delegate it, or fake it. This is one thing you can't pay someone else to do for you.

True influence and persuasion comes from the inside.

Fortunately, there is a four-step process that makes things easy for you. It applies to all four Dimensions of The Influence Code™ and it breaks down into four simple steps.

1. **Understand** your own Natural Style and Communication Code
2. **Recognize** other people's Code (people reading)
3. **Appreciate** the value other people bring to the table
4. **Persuade** others and motivate them to action by adapting <u>your</u> Code to <u>theirs</u>!

Ultimately, adaptation is where the power is.

Sometimes people are forced to adapt in order to survive. Sometimes they choose to adapt in order to succeed. Others need to adapt in order to win someone over to their point of view, or to get rapid results from their team.

Successful adaptation means you need to know where you're starting from and what you're adapting to. This simple four-step process is what will give you control over that adaptation with priceless insight into yourself and your strengths. This insight is what will help you to know when and where to use your Natural Style, and where to adapt.

So let's take a look under the hood and see how you can make each of these four steps work for you with online persuasion.

It Starts With Your Code!

As we mentioned earlier, influencing and persuading others starts with learning to influence yourself first.

If you don't understand what your own Natural Style and Communication Code is, how can you ever adapt to anyone else's? You're lost from the start.

It's like when one of my friends who recently visited us in Hawaii got lost on his way to our place.

We had planned in advance to get together while he was out here on vacation, and on the first trip out to our place, he gets lost.

I get the inevitable call, *"Hey JP! I think I'm lost. How do I get to your place?"*

I ask my friend where he is, and he says, *"I don't know, but there's a beach over here on my right."*

Laughing I say, *"Hmmmm... we're on an island in the middle of the Pacific and your landmark is a beach! That helps!"* Fortunately, he's still in high spirits from all the sunshine and fresh air he's taking in, and laughs with me.

"*Seriously,*" I say, "*go ask someone which beach you're near.*"

Of course, the "someone" I hear him ask is some local girl, and after a fleeting (and feeble) attempt at flirting, he's back on the phone. He tells me he's at Pipeline Beach.

It's only at that point that I can give him directions on how to get to our house, because I have a starting point from where he is at right now.

It's the same thing with persuasion. You can't establish rapport, influence, or persuasion with another person until you adapt to his or her Code. You need both your own starting point and where the other person is at in order to connect the Codes together.

The faster you can break someone else's Code, the faster you can connect.

You can't adapt to another person's Communication Code until you know your own.

This is the number one reason so many people are lost when they try to influence and persuade others using proven strategies they read in a book or learned at a seminar. They won't get the results they want using more advanced persuasion strategies until they know their own Natural Style and Code.

STEP 1. WHAT'S YOUR COMMUNICATION CODE?

Each of us has a natural way of dealing with:

- Problems, risks and challenges
- People and interactions
- Pace and changes
- Procedures and rules

Without giving you an actual scientific assessment, we'll have to do this subjectively. But I'm sure you'll get the idea.

So how do YOU "deal?" Let's see. Grab a pen and complete the following quick exercise.

Next are four statements. Read each of the four statements and rank them in order of your personal preference, one through four.

Start by ranking the statement you feel most strongly about with a one, and rank the others in order through the number four, which should be the statement you least relate to.

C   I like working in an environment with a set system of rules and procedures. Details are critical!

D   I feel energized and motivated when facing a big challenge or risk. Bring it on!

Rank: ____   Rank: ____

S   I prefer a daily routine that has a slow, steady pace without a lot of sudden changes. Slow and Steady.

I   I love making people laugh, being around people, and being "the life of the party." Let's have fun!

Rank: ____   Rank: ____

Which choice got your highest score? Circle the letter to the left of your highest ranking statement.

Here's what each letter represents and some adjectives to help confirm you're on the right track.

- **D** stands for the **Driver Style**

    Descriptive adjectives for the Driver Style:

    Ambitious, forceful, decisive, strong-willed, independent, goal-oriented.

- **I** stands for the **Influencer Style**

    Descriptive adjectives for the Influencer Style:

    Magnetic, enthusiastic, friendly, demonstrative, political

- **S** stands for the **Steady Style**

    Descriptive adjectives for the Steady Style:

    Patient, predictable, reliable, steady, relaxed, modest

- **C** stands for the **Compliant Style**

    Descriptive adjectives for the Compliant Style:

    Conscientious, diplomatic, analytical, precise, perfectionist

Now that you're getting an idea of what your Natural Communication Style may be, let's move to step two and start looking at other people.

Step 2. Recognizing Other People's Style

What if you always knew exactly what to say at the right time, every time, to every person you meet? Sound impossible?

For the seasoned influencer, this is not only possible, but it's practical, too. When you use the right words with the right people at the right time, it's incredibly rewarding seeing people's faces light up. Or when someone's attitude changes right in front of you for the better, as a result of your words and actions chosen correctly.

Whether it brings you closer to your goals, or gets you out of a sticky situation, you'll get more of what you want and less of what you don't when you recognize the needs of other people, and meet their needs using their Code.

Being able to influence and persuade others is a soft-skill largely overlooked in high schools, colleges, and universities across America. There's no required communication course to graduate, yet it's clearly one of the most important skills you can learn.

Whether it's securing your first job, or landing a major contract, if you don't relate to the person who has decision-making power over your destiny, you're doomed. (No wonder so many people think success is based more on luck than skill.)

The power to influence and persuade resides in your hands. Whether you choose to learn to harness and apply this power is completely up to you.

If you're passionate about your product, service or platform, if you truly believe that you have a solution that the world needs – you owe it to yourself and others to learn how to persuasively get your message across.

Cracking Other People's Communication Code™

Let's look at some secrets of the best influencers of our time – from President Reagan or Clinton, to Oprah, and Governor Schwarzenegger.

Knowing and utilizing what the superstars of influence and persuasion use, will give you the edge over your competitors. You'll also experience a more enjoyable personal life, as you learn to get more of what you want, and less of what you don't – with the people you already love and trust on a daily basis.

The secret starts with listening, watching, and observing.

The way these and other persuasion masters WOW crowds, is by knowing individuals. By learning how to connect and build rapport with one individual, and practicing the technique over and over again; otherwise normal people become masters of influence and persuasion.

Sadly, most people do not listen at all. They are so anxious to get what they have to say out of their head in a conversation that when the other person takes a breath, they're ready to pounce like a hungry housecat on a scurrying mouse.

It doesn't matter whether it's in person or online, it's the same scenario that plays out with the non-influencing person. If he does manage to control himself, and let the other person talk, he's either busy thinking of what he'll say next, or listening to what's being said through his own Natural Style. He's not listening in order to discover the other person's style. This is a fatal flaw, and made more often than we like to see.

Observation and knowing what to look for is what allows persuasion masters to successfully adapt to and connect with so many people from different walks of life.

Whether your goal is to influence influencers, offline or online, you will need to begin by looking for the same four key indicators. Fortunately, these indicators will all be obvious – even to the untrained eye or ear.

In the following matrix (figure 12-1) you'll see the same four styles that you just looked at in step one.

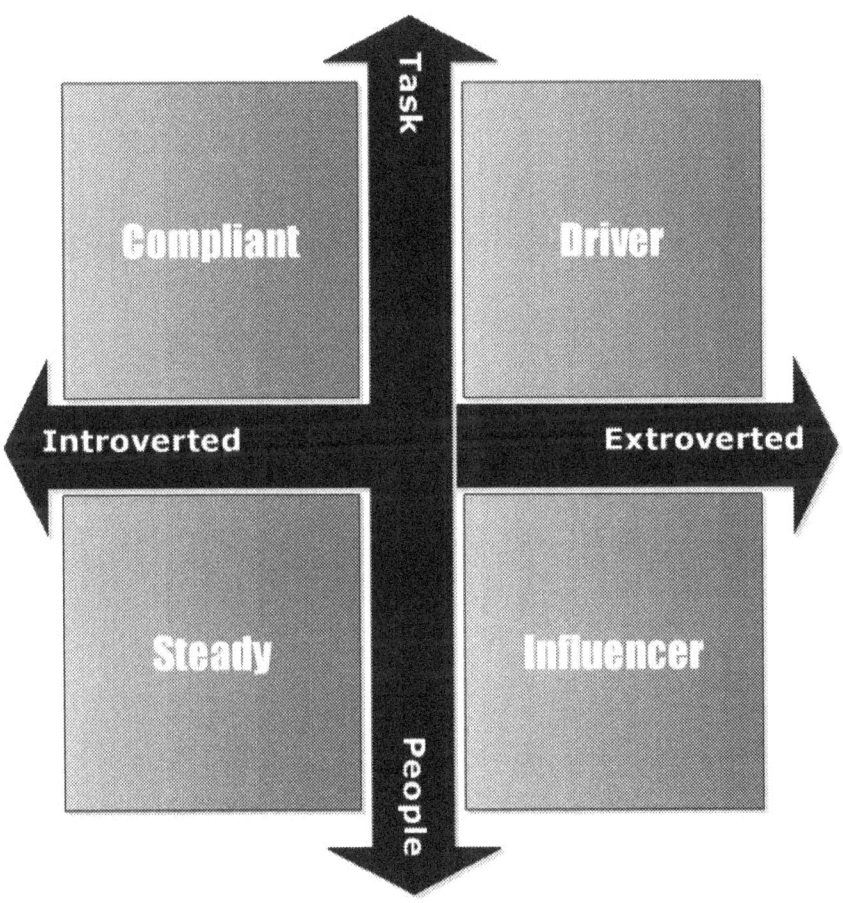

Figure 12-1

As you look at this matrix, pay attention to the horizontal and vertical divisions.

The horizontal division shows a varying range of intensity when observing extroverted behavior to introverted behavior. The vertical division shows the range of task-focused behavior to people-focused behavior.

By carefully listening to what people say, reading what people write, or seeing how they respond to questions, you can quickly get an initial feel as to whether a person is task or people focused.

If a person seems more focused on tasks and results in the way he talks or writes, there's a good chance that his primary Natural Style falls in the upper half of the matrix, making it a good possibility that he's either a Driver or Compliant Style Communicator.

If a person seems to focus more on people in her answers, writing, or general conversation, then she falls in the lower half of the matrix, making it likely that her primary Natural Style is an Influencer or Steady Communicator.

Observing whether a person is more introverted or extroverted can be a little easier offline since you can watch his or her body language and hear the tone and pace of their speech, but people leave clues online too.

The good thing about online observation is that you have a lot more time to look for indicators to give you clues into a person's communication style.

Even with that time and knowing where to look to learn more about a person, you still need to know what you're looking for. So let's give you a big jumpstart on that right now.

Some of the most important clues left by people online are their:

- General profile orientation
- Writing style
- Conversational tone
- Favorite books or movies they list in their profile
- Speed at which they buy-in to new things or topics in forums

All these are easier to see and hear in the New Media Marketplace with blogs, Podcasts, comments, social networks, forums, etc.

In the following chart (figure 12-2) we've highlighted the top characteristics for each of these five categories to give you clues for all four Natural Communication Styles in the people you network with online.

Online Identifiers

Compliant	Driver
Orientation: information & procedures	**Orientation**: results & efficiency
Writing style: direct, to the point, more technical with data and research	**Writing style**: to the point, results & ROI, big picture, directive
Conversational tone: direct, questioning, clarifying	**Conversational tone**: direct, very little chit-chat
Tends to read: non-fiction, research materials, technical & technology related	**Tends to read**: success oriented & result improvement materials, non-fiction
Buy in: slow, prefers proven & tested products	**Buy in**: quick decision, prefers new & unique products

Steady	Influencer
Orientation: emotionally detached but trusting	**Orientation**: fun & experience
Writing style: long with lots of info, sharing, contributory	**Writing style**: more wordy, warm people focus, can appear disorganized at times
Conversational tone: warm, conversational, friendly, concerned	**Conversational tone**: personal, verbose, & sometimes humorous
Tends to read: people stories, fiction and non-fiction	**Tends to read**: fiction, self-improvement
Buy in: slow, prefers traditional products	**Buy in**: quick, leans toward 'showy' products

Figure 12-2

Using this chart and the matrix shown in figure 12-1 together, will give you a huge jump-start in identifying the style of a Tribal Influencer, or anyone else you'd like to quickly gain favor with. You'll be well on your way to breaking their entire Communication Code.

Remember these are only tendencies that indicate what a person's primary style MAY be. This is simply a starting point for your interaction with a person.

As you learn more about the Influence Code™ and communicate with the person through blog comments, emails, online networking, or phone and in-person meetings – you'll be able to fine-tune your subjective analysis of his or her style. As you learn more, you'll be able to adapt more effectively.

Coaching Tip: More and more, audio capability is being added to online chats, forums, interactive teleconferences, and online networking events. Do yourself a favor, invest in a set of speakers for your computer, a quality microphone, and headset in order to participate in these types of events; they will give you the edge to uncover even more clues into people's communication styles.

Finding The Info You Need Online

- *How would it be if you could have a communication manual on the people you work with?*

- *What if you had the equivalent to a "code book" for every person you interacted with online?*

- *What if you knew the secret access codes to the buttons you need to push in order to get better results with your clients and prospects?*

Unless you can get a copy of someone's actual Communication Code report, you'll need to speculate on his or her style as accurately as possible. We've already given you ways to start doing that in this chapter.

But how do you find the information online that will help you determine their Natural Style?

You can identify the main communication style of another person after spending a minimum amount of time online digging into her online Web presence, and by "Googling" her. (Now, we didn't say drooling over her, we said Googling her, which simply means you type in her name in Google.com and see what comes up that matches her profile.)

These two types of research tools, Googling, and reviewing someone's online Web presence will give you plenty to start working with – if they're truly an online influencer.

Let's take a closer look at these two methods of research that are at your fingertips.

1. WEB PRESENCE

As we mentioned earlier in this book, there is a big difference between a Web site and a Web Presence.

Most people you'll be dealing with in the New Media Marketplace understand the difference. You'll be able to find tons of info, writings, and commentary that will give you insight into a person's Communication Code and Natural Style.

The first place to look will be her blog (business and/or personal.) Thanks to her writing and content, you'll be able to collect a tremendous amount of information in terms of nearly every characteristic we covered in figure 12-2.

From there you'll usually find links to the online social networks she belongs to. The profile pages on these social networks can often provide a wealth of information from different perspectives.

If she's a Tribal Influencer, you'll often find a Clan or Band that she's personally organized or regularly participates in. This can be inside a formal social network, or "outside" and independent.

Some of these groups may be closed to the general public, but with other groups, you'll be able to easily join the group and begin to participate. This is going to give you even more insight since you'll be able to observe and research complete interactions and conversations.

Another targeted way to research a person's Web presence is using a "blog specific" search engine like Technorati.com, Feedster.com, or IceRocket.com. Searches on these specialized engines may lead you to posts made by the person you're researching or by others that you would otherwise be unable to find.

2. *"Googling"*

If you're trying to initiate a relationship and influence someone who is still operating online using a Web Marketing 1.0 approach, then you'll need to rely on standard search engines.

Googling is a term that describes how you do an Internet search for the people you have met or would like to meet. With these searches you can see what other people are saying about them, and what they're all about. Not to mention digging up any criminal background on would-be suitors for the young, urban professional in the dating scene.

All you do is go to Google.com, Yahoo.com, Ask.com or any other search engine of your choosing. Type in the person's name and see what comes up.

Be sure to enter his/her name both with and without quotes around his/her name. Cross-reference at least two or three search engines always including Google.com and Yahoo.com for the most thorough results. (Google and Yahoo use very different search algorithms and can give dramatically different results on a search.)

In the results you may find articles this person authored, places he or she has presented, press releases on his or her company, or charitable events he or she sponsors.

All the information you gather here can be run through the filters we covered earlier in step two and will give you a great starting point for influencing the influencer.

Once you've got step one and two under your belt, you may be tempted to jump ahead to adaptation. With practice, adaptation will become subconscious and very natural for you. But for now, step three is critical, as it's where the necessary practice comes from.

STEP 3. APPRECIATING THE NATURAL STYLE OF OTHERS

You've been introduced to the four basic Communication Styles that the majority of people fall into. You know that you need to communicate with people according to <u>their</u> Code. Now, you'll learn how to make your adaptation easy, accurate, and more meaningful.

Masters of influence and persuasion rarely (if ever) have their actions perceived as "contrived." Their words, actions, and conversations always come across as authentic. And that's what you want.

To do this, you must honestly appreciate what a person brings to the table when they have a Communication Style that's different from your own.

What we've found through experience is that people pick this skill up the fastest when they focus on people they already know, and begin appreciating their strengths and attractive qualities.

So let's do a quick four-minute exercise right now that will put you on the road to authentic adaptation.

Start by thinking about the people in your life that you know well. Identify three people for each of the following four main styles that you believe closely matches the descriptions for each Communication Code.

Write their names down in the lines provided on the following pages, according to the communication style you see them most accurately fitting into.

Then, beside their name, write which adjective or adjectives you associate with that person. On the line under each name, write down the approach you currently use to get results with that particular person.

D = Driver Code:

Identify and list three people in your personal or professional life who can be described as **ambitious, forceful, decisive, strong-willed, independent and goal-oriented.**

1. _____

_____

_____

2. _____
_____
_____

3. _____
_____
_____

I = Influencing Code:

Identify and list three people in your personal or professional life who can be described as **magnetic, enthusiastic, friendly, demonstrative and political.**

1. _____
_____
_____

2. _____
_____
_____

3. _____
_____
_____

S = Steadiness Code:

Identify and list three people in your personal or professional life who can be described as **patient, predictable, reliable, steady, relaxed and modest.**

1. _____

2. _____

3. _____

C = Compliant Code:

Identify and list three people in your personal or professional life who can be described as **conscientious, diplomatic, analytical, precise, or a perfectionist.**

1. _____

2. _____

3. _____
_____
_____

Think about each of these people who are already in your life. Think about their strong points and what they bring to the table.

Sure, some family members or in-laws may be tough. ☺ But if you really think about it, there are some strengths each of them have.

This is a critical thing to remember for long-term success in adapting your Communication Code to influence and persuade – you don't necessarily need to "like" everything about the people you're adapting to.

To get the results you want, you simply need to appreciate some strengths they have in order to remove any judgment you may unconsciously carry about them. With that appreciation, you can adapt authentically and are much more likely to get the results you want.

Otherwise, people will smell judgment like a dog can smell fear. They'll sense it, and want to be as far away from you as possible. But if they honestly feel you like them, or can appreciate their strengths, they'll be attracted to you like a magnet.

Step 4. Persuasion through adaptation

Most people communicate with others in the same old way they've been communicating since grammar school.

They give no thought to the fact that we're each created uniquely, that we all have very different backgrounds and experiences that shape our preferences and judgments. So most people default to "what comes naturally."

Sure, communicating in your Natural Style may feel "comfortable," but is it really the best way to communicate with every person you interact with?

You wouldn't go to your best friend's black-tie wedding in the same clothes you find "comfortable" to wear watching TV at home or going to the beach. Would you?

In the same way, you shouldn't enter a conversation (offline or online) wearing the same Communication Style that's most comfortable for you. You must adapt appropriately.

To do this, you must first observe the unspoken cultural "rules" of the event and pick up on the communication clues of individual conversations.

Take networking for example. What type of communication is the culture of the "room" expecting? How are the people already engaged in a conversation interacting? What are the styles of the people engaged?

Don't just rush in with your own agenda and expect other people to adapt to you. It isn't going to happen!

Seek first to understand who the main players are before you try to be heard yourself. This applies offline and online.

The best thing about networking online, compared to networking in-person, is that you get to check people out before you walk up and say, "Aloha!"

Offline networking events don't afford you this luxury. Who knows what dark shadowy figure you'll be cornered by at an in-person event.

There's no way of knowing whether you have something they need or vice versa until you introduce yourself and begin talking with them. By then, it may be too late. You may be sucked into a black hole of boredom and time-sucking despair, sometimes even without your invitation.

Chances are, you've been to an event where you got stuck with a time vampire. Someone who wasted your time talking about his business and how great he is the entire time, without ever even asking you what you do, or if you could even use his service or not.

I still have flashbacks about one such nightmarish event at a business networking function in Manhattan. No sooner did I sign in and pointlessly paste the silly little nametag on my suit jacket when I was approached by a "close talker." He wanted to sell me advertising on placemats in diners everywhere from Manhattan to Redbank.

What the heck?!?

Did I just step off 54th Street onto the planet of the clueless?

My nametag says I'm a Business Coach. He had barely heard two words out of my mouth before introducing himself, so he didn't have a clue that I have a strong Driver Style and can't stand people who babble on and on in general – never mind people who babble on about things I don't care about.

Why would I ever be remotely interested in advertising on a placemat?

Obviously, he was too close to my face to notice that the strap for my briefcase was falling off my right shoulder, sliding down to my right elbow, while my purse on my left shoulder also needed to be adjusted after paying for the event.

Talk about clueless!

Thank God I had my New York game face on and was quickly able to extricate myself from that dark bottomless pit with the first familiar face I saw.

Whew! Close one!

My partner describes these people accurately as "time vampires." These are people who don't care what they're saying, as long as they have someone to talk to.

Sadly, many of these types of people don't know why they're not making any connections. They don't realize that they could create radically different results if they only learned the four-step process we're introducing to you in this chapter.

With online networking, this is completely avoidable. You get to review people's online profile before entering into a conversation or sending them an email to introduce yourself.

If you have a Web presence, people can in turn check you out, see what you each have in common, and begin the relationship ten steps ahead of a normal, in-person event.

Needless to say, online networking has very quickly become my preferred way to meet new people and build relationships. "Mr. Placemat Guy" will never bother me again with online networking!

Ok, now that you have one example of how the application of one's "Natural Style" without adaptation can be extremely harmful – let's take a look at how to make adaptation easy.

Opening The Door To Effective Communication

Before you begin building a relationship and learning more about a person's Communication Code, you need to get your proverbial foot in the door.

If you're trying to influence an influencer, your first contact is even more important because very often they are busy people who you're trying to connect with, and you need to respect their time, if you're going to even come close to influencing them effectively.

Whether your goal is to get your point across, communicate an idea, or persuade someone that your solution is the best answer to his or her problem – you'll need to know how to open the door to the other person's preferred Communication Style in order to be heard.

In the next chapter, you'll be able to create your own cheat sheet to begin adapting to other people for maximum influence and persuasion.

The Art And Science Of Effectively Persuading Your Target Audience And The Masses

chapter thirteen

"They say we offer simple answers to complex problems. Well, perhaps there is a simple answer — not an easy answer — but simple."

– Ronald Reagan in his October 27, 1964 speech *"A Time for Choosing"*

》》Radio show hosts love when we predict elections in the United States. From governors to Presidents, we always begin our analysis by looking at the statistics of the four different communication styles that people categorically fit into.

This allows us to see which candidate the majority of people will naturally relate to, and which candidates will need to adapt in order to have any chance of winning.

Learn how you can best communicate, motivate, sell to and interact with people of all four styles, and you'll not only be the most popular with your prospects, clients or voters, you'll also be way ahead of your competitors who are still trying to "wing it" by communicating the same way they did when they were in high school.

The following four examples will relate back to the four Communication Styles we just reviewed, giving you additional demographics, and psychographics for you to be aware of, when analyzing your target audience. Feel free to refer back to the examples and figures we just shared.

Now, begin creating your own list of Do's and Don'ts for each type of influencer you are communicating with or selling to in your business – either online or offline.

#1: Dealing with DRIVERS like David

First let's look at the "High Achiever" behavioral style that 18% of the population fall into.

David will represent the Driver Style in this example.

David is a person who is ambitious and results-oriented. He is known for being direct, forceful, independent and goal-oriented. He got to where he is in business by being 100% focused on the tasks at hand.

People will tell you that, "You always know where you stand with David."

When communicating with someone who has a similar style to David, you will want to follow a different strategy than you would with the majority of the population.

COACHES PERSUASION SECRETS:

Here are a few pointers to get you started.

DO:

- ☑ Be clear, specific, brief and to the point.
- ☑ Think about what matters most to him when talking about strategies. (What may be important to you may not be the main focus for him.)
- ☑ Stick to business. He's not a fan of beating around the bush, and has little time for chit-chat. Getting right to the business topic at hand is not considered rude to David, it's considered time and business-savvy.
- ☑ Be prepared with support material in a concise, well-organized "package."

When you adhere to these basic tips, you will not only be able to get your message across, but you'll also pave the way for future business relations with David. He will respect you as a professional who cares about results.

DON'T:

Never get caught doing the following:

- ☒ Don't talk about things that are not relevant to the issue at hand.
- ☒ Don't mess around with unimportant or irrelevant issues.

- Don't leave loopholes in your conversation, argument or presentation.
- Don't talk about cloudy issues. Figure out the point to any subject at hand, and determine what action must be taken next in order to move forward.
- Never appear disorganized – or you will lose him immediately, not to mention his respect for you in future business dealings.

WARNING: *If you are a sales person, and you try a traditional approach with someone like David, (perhaps the same approach that works for 80% of your customers) you'll quickly find yourself wondering why he left your store or Web site and never returned.*

#2 Influencing the Influencers like ISABELLA:

Next, let's look at the Influencing behavioral style that 28% of the population represents. You'll quickly be able to identify people you work with who share this style, because they're the most gregarious and outgoing of all the styles.

Isabella will represent the Influencing Style in this example.

Isabella is a person who is enthusiastic, magnetic, friendly, demonstrative and political. She enjoys socializing with others and welcomes personal dialogue about what is going on in your life.

People describe her as being a friendly, fun-loving person who doesn't really have any enemies.

Some people have mistakenly read her enthusiasm for being "phony" or "superficial," but this is generally not the case – especially for people who know her best.

Isabella naturally trusts people, and can easily open up to strangers, whether traveling in an elevator with them, or welcoming them to a new environment. That's why she has lots of friends.

COACHES PERSUASION SECRETS:

When communicating with someone who has a similar Communication Code as Isabella, remember to adhere to the following key points when you get together online or face-to-face.

DO:

☑ Provide a warm, open, and friendly environment that allows for chit-chat.

☑ Ask "feeling" questions in order to discover her opinions or comments on what you are talking about.

☑ Make your conversations or blog posts fun and entertaining.

Let her know in some way that you like her as a person, and enjoy talking with her. If she comments on your blog, be sure you reply to her directly.

☑ Focus on rapport building and developing a real relationship with her – not on details and research studies.

This is often indicated by the amount of time spent independently with her, or allowing her to talk with you about something she is interested in.

Send her a private message (PM) when you're in membership forums when she posts. Discover what makes her tick, and she'll reveal more than any of the other communication styles combined.

If she likes you, she will listen to what you have to say, or read what you send her – provided you give her a lot of bulleted lists and white space.

If she doesn't like you, she will discard what you send her, because she will have a more difficult time trusting what you have to say.

DON'T:

Never get caught doing any of the following:

- ✗ Don't be curt, short, or tight-lipped.
- ✗ Don't give one-word answers or statements. (Instead, elaborate using a story, metaphor or example to bring your point across in a way she'll remember positively.)
- ✗ Don't try to control the conversation, or cut her off. (Remember to allow her to talk, and allow her to finish the stories she starts. Just don't let her get off track.)
- ✗ Don't focus solely on facts and figures. (Allow this information to be included in the written material you "refer to" and then leave this information behind for her to reference when you're finished networking with her online.)

WARNING: *If you are a sales person, and you try to cut directly to business at hand without some friendly conversation, you may find resistance at first.*

Just be sure that you do not take advantage of Isabella's naturally trusting nature. If you take her needs into account, and only sell her what she needs/wants, you'll have her as a customer for life, and a stark-raving-fan!

If you sell her something that is ineffective, or not what she needs, she'll never trust you as a business professional, and will find someone else the next time she needs the product or service you offer.

#3: Strengthening Relationships with Steady Serena

Now let's look at the Steady, Reliable behavioral style that the majority of the population fill at a whopping 40%!

If politicians or leaders don't bring these people on their side, they don't stand a chance in winning.

Serena will represent the Steady Style in this example.

Serena is a person who is patient, reliable, relaxed, and modest. People get along with Serena as she craves an environment free from conflict and disagreement.

The team she surrounds herself with agrees that she can be predictable in how she wants things done. She supports the leader of a membership organization, forum or networking association, or because she believes the membership's purpose supports people.

COACHES PERSUASION SECRETS:

Here are a few pointers to get you started with the majority of the worldwide population – over 40% of people – who relate to people like Serena.

DO:

When communicating with someone who is similar to Serena, remember to adhere to the following key points when you get together online.

- ☑ Begin your interactions or group networking events, with a personal comment – break the ice before discussing business issues or tele-class topics.

- ☑ Present your case softly, in a non-threatening manner.

- ☑ Ask her "How" questions to draw out her opinions or feedback on your blog or in your network.

- ☑ End every interaction assuring her position with you is on good terms.

DON'T:

Don't ever get caught doing the following, or you'll regret it for a long time to come, and you'll certainly lose any popularity contest you're going after online, not to mention profits from a large crowd.

- ☒ Don't be domineering or demanding if you want to be heard.

If you join a networking event online, allow her voice to be heard, before you start sharing all your knowledge about a specific subject.

- ☒ Don't expect her to respond quickly to your posts or topics posted if she's a new member. Give her plenty of time to warm up to the group.

- ☒ Allow her to get involved with the decision making process or at least explain the rationale behind any changes needing to be made within your online networking association group.

WARNING: *If you are a sales person, and try to push her into making a decision before she has time to weigh out the pros and cons, you're going to lose her trust. Be sincere and warm. Allow her to ask questions before she makes her buying decision. Trust me, if you invest the time today, and she is satisfied with your product or service, you'll almost guarantee that you'll have her as your loyal customer for life, and she'll forgive a multitude of mistakes if she truly likes you!*

Serena is loyal and willing to stick in a relationship much longer than she probably should, but she would rather deal with a less than ideal product or service than make a change to an unknown company that scares her even more.

Be careful, because she holds her hurt feelings inside, and doesn't say anything at first. (The saying "the straw that broke the camel's back" relates to Serena's style of dealing with frustrations.)

She'll be the customer you never hear a complaint from. Instead, she'll simply leave when someone else wins her trust and favor, and you'll never know why.

Solicit her feedback. Listen to her opinions, and watch your sales soar.

When you get feedback from all the Serena's on your list, you're bound to tap into a few secrets that will drive more people to your company, product or service, because she has a pulse on what the people need, want, and desire.

#4 Conform to Compliant Clarks

Finally, let's look at the Compliant behavioral style, that a mere 14% of the population fall into. Just keep in mind, that even though the minority of the population has this style, if this is your demographic, it means all the difference to your success or failure if you satisfy this type of clientele.

Clark will represent the Compliant Style in this example.

Clark is a person who is dependent, neat, conservative, compliant to the rules and procedures and quality conscious.

People around the water cooler will tell you he tends to be a perfectionist and pays close attention to detail. He'll see a speck of lint on your pants from across the hall. He'll be the first person to email you to inform you that you have a spelling or typographical error on your Web site or blog.

Clark is extremely task-oriented. When given specific instructions as to what needs to be done, he can be relied upon to rise to the occasion. Clark's primary concern on the job is ensuring that the quality and integrity of the projects he is responsible for fulfill a superior rating.

When communicating with someone who is similar to Clark, remember to adhere to the following key points when you meet online.

COACHES PERSUASION SECRETS:

Here are a few pointers to get you started.

DO:

☑ Prepare your pitch in advance. (Don't make careless mistakes when it comes to the details of your offer – he'll see it as a fatal flaw in the entire product or service you're offering.)

☑ Stick to business. (Don't stray from the topic.)

Effectively Persuading Your Target Audience | 237

☑ Be accurate and realistic. (Don't make promises that are impossible to keep. He sees right through them!)

☑ Be sure to have all the details about your product or offer before presenting it to him.

☑ When possible, show him tables, charts and graphs that depict how your product far surpasses your competitor's product.

☑ Do some research for him, and give him as much detail to support your claims as possible.

☑ Be polished, professional, and prepared for him to correct you, if something you say or do is not clearly or perfectly presented.

When you adhere to the above guidelines, he will respect you as a professional who cares about quality, and will buy from you when he's good and ready.

DON'T:

Never get caught doing the following:

✗ Don't be giddy, too casual, informal or loud.

✗ Don't try and push too hard for him to make a decision today. (Allow him to think about all the details involved and the implications that come into play.)

✗ Avoid disorganization or messy demeanor, presentation or materials. (If there are spelling/grammatical errors, be prepared to hear about it from him, and nod accordingly. Assure him that errors will be corrected promptly.)

WARNING: *If you are a salesperson, don't use "fluffy" words with someone like Clark. NEVER, ever "embellish" on your product or service. Instead, stick to the truth about the quality of your product or service, even if it means admitting some of the weak points. After all, if you don't he sure will.*

You can rest assured; extensive research was executed before he put one foot in your showroom/store, blog or Web site. In fact, you may want to appeal to his expertise and allow him to "do the talking."

As he begins to tell you about your own product — LET HIM! By all means, give him time and space; he'll probably compare and contrast all the different products you offer and actually sell himself based on *his own criteria* — not yours.

COACHES NOTE:

Remember, our Communication Styles and preferences are as unique as our fingerprints. Keep in mind that there are over 40,000 possible combinations that can be mapped out as a result of the responses to the assessments we use with our clients.

The above four examples are designed to give you an easy to remember overview of the four main styles that the majority of people fall into. If you're looking to build powerful teams that work together towards a common goal, you'll want to take this knowledge to the next level. (More in-depth analysis and exploration will be covered in the next book we write.)

In the meantime, join us in the conversation at www.TheInfluence-Code.com we'd love to hear how you apply the above tips and persuasion secrets. We're also happy to answer any questions you may have as a result of reading this book.

To Do Or Not To Do

Sometimes after doing your research, you'll be pretty confident about a person's Natural Style, so focusing on what TO DO is easier. Other times you may still not have enough information to determine what a person's Natural Style is, so it's helpful to focus on what NOT to do.

Remember, this is only a starting point.

As you begin your communication with a person, you need to continue to observe and adapt on an ongoing basis. With every personal interaction you'll learn more that will help you determine his/her Natural Style and Communication Code.

With practice, you will influence the influencers with ease. In the New Media Marketplace, this is a skill that will set you head and shoulders above your competition.

Once you've got some experience and feel confident that you've got some momentum on the principles laid out in this chapter, then you can kick things up a notch with the unique, interactive chapters on iBuzz, iBrand, iConnect, and iProfit that follow.

But be sure you have this chapter down before moving ahead.

Reread it once or twice. Nothing in marketing with New Media is more important than your ability to influence and persuade the Tribal Influencers, and in turn the entire Tribe.

Secrets To Influence And Persuade The Masses

Today, the most successful people are those who can adapt to any environment. They know their Do's and Don'ts rules, and can persuade the masses.

Former President Bill Clinton had this gift.

I still remember getting totally ticked off as I tried to get from one Rutgers Campus to another for a Psychology class. I was stuck in unbelievable traffic because the President of the United States was speaking at our college that day.

Thanks to the detours, I got to class late and was pretty frustrated. I had a few choice words to say about the President's motorcade and that sparked a heated political conversation in the classroom. The professor just sat back and observed for a bit, then she stepped in and said something about the then brand new President I'll never forget.

"No matter what political party you favor, Bill Clinton has this nearly magical ability of touching you when you're in the audience."

I was shocked at a party that weekend when a Republican friend of mine said virtually the same thing about how she felt when she saw him speak at Rutgers that week. My friend compared the event to the same feeling you get when you go to a rock concert, and described the feeling of the room as "electrified." She also said Clinton had a way of "energizing you to get involved in politics."

Apparently, he knew it was a mixed crowd that came out to hear him speak and knew how to adapt accordingly.

Republicans, Democrats and Independents alike came to hear what the new President had to say about the countries' affairs. He stayed away from topics that would divide the audience, and instead focused on things that every human being would agree on – provided they had a pulse.

Sharing stories was a powerful influencing strategy that both Reagan and Clinton used in order to influence and persuade the audience. Oprah's daily show seems to guarantee there will be some

Effectively Persuading Your Target Audience | 241

type of tearjerker story designed to trigger an emotional response in the viewer or listener.

Regardless of the messenger delivering the story, the feelings stirred up from a powerful story well told, will still impact you as the listener. Like my college friend, what she remembered from her encounter with the President, is the way she felt when she was in his presence.

Experts in Neuro-Linguistic Programming (NLP) define this technique as "Associative Conditioning." What it boils down to is similar to what happens when you go to a movie.

You get engaged in the story line of the movie. You forget about the troubles and stresses that you left at the office for the night. Just when the climax of the movie takes place, you hear Celine Dion belting out one of the most melodic, emotion-charged songs of her career.

You weep. You grab the stack of napkins, pretending you need them for your greasy popcorn eating hands. Your heart goes out to the characters on screen. Thinking of all the real life people who experienced the same thing that's being displayed so masterfully on the silver screen in front of you.

You now associate all the positive feelings you're experiencing with the movie you're watching to the song you're hearing.

The next day as you're driving to your child's soccer match, Celine Dion's song, *My Heart Will Go On,* comes on the radio. It's the same song you heard during the climax of the movie the night before.

Tears well up in your eyes, and the same feelings you had sitting in the movie theater come rushing back. This is Associative Conditioning. You associate the same feelings with a Celine Dion song as you did with the most emotional parts of the movie.

Chapter Thirteen

This same strategy is used not just by politicians who constantly need the edge over their opponents, but also by the Motivational Superstars who are traveling around the U.S. on the Speaker's Circuit, pulling between $100,000 to $500,000 or more, directly from the pocketbooks of the audience in just one engagement

Knowing this secret alone will become one of your most valuable assets – even if you're not running for the Presidency just yet. ☺

The Ten Commandments Of New Media Marketing Success

chapter fourteen

"Read the directions and directly you will be directed in the right direction."

– *The doorknob,* Alice in Wonderland

》》Ok, so they aren't really *commandments* in the true sense of the word. They weren't written in stone by the finger of God and you won't be struck down by lightning if you break any of them. In fact, we're big rule breakers.

What's important is that when you can learn from those who've gone before you, it'll give you a huge edge over your competitors who don't know any better.

Use these Ten Commandments as guiding principles or laws for successfully marketing with New Media. If you break them once, you may not get caught. If you break them over and over again, you'll feel it where it hurts – your pocketbook, or bottom line.

These commandments are garnered from more than 3,000 hours of research and testing, as well as our own personal experiences. One piece of advice my Dad gave me when I was 12 has always stood out for me over the years, "Don't just learn from other people's success stories; you'll learn more from other people's mistakes, so you won't have to make them yourself."

We made a lot of mistakes ourselves over the last two years before we came up with these ten easy-to-follow laws designed to help you further develop your New Media mindset — while helping you avoid needless mistakes:

1. **Thou shalt be a market thinker, not a product pusher.**

    This means you are going to be part of the marketplace without being engulfed by it. The goal is to look for problems people have and solve them.

    Contrast that with the typical salesperson or traditional advertising campaign – all about pushing a product or service, with no regard for the end user.

2. **Thou shalt participate and profit without becoming an evangelist.**

    Observe, participate, and leverage the New Media Marketplace without getting caught up in the hype or the technology. You want to always stand guard at the door of your mind while participating. Be careful not to get dragged into the sheep pen again. Many evangelists tend to be hammers and, therefore, see every problem as a nail.

Just like any other idea or technology, when enough people get going in a line, it's just like a flock of sheep headed back to the pen. You need to stay outside of that herd mentality.

Instead, constantly innovate with lateral thinking, and continue to have an independent mindset.

3. **Thou shalt keep thy marketing an ongoing conversation.**

   Once a conversation takes place, a relationship is formed. You nurture that relationship and you build rapport. That rapport leads to trust, and eventually to influence and persuasion. Not influence and persuasion in the way those terms have been bastardized by political correctness, but in a good and healthy way that exists in any relationship.

   A conversation can occur one-on-one – or as we're talking about here, one-on-one x 10,000 or one-on-one x 100,000.

   Seth Godin forecast this leveraged type of networking in 1999, and most companies STILL haven't gotten it. Marketing is permission; it's not interruption.

   Interruption marketing (the way old-school advertisers and marketers are still trying to do it) doesn't work anymore. Marketing is permission and permission is only gained after engaging and listening.

   The Cluetrain Manifesto is a great book for exploring the concept of the marketplace being a conversation. It primarily focuses on large corporations and the corporate world, trying to get them to understand in their own type of language how they need to change and adapt to this new marketplace. It's a conversation and conversation leads to connection, rapport, and trust.

4. **Thou shalt understand your target audience and honor their wants, needs, and desires.**

    This is just good solid Marketing 101. It's surprising how many business owners don't have a clear and specific description of who their target market is.

    Your target audience is dying to tell you what they want, but if you don't know exactly who they are, you can't use New Media to make life easy.

5. **Thou shalt listen, learn, observe, and adapt.**

    This is easier than ever before because the New Media Marketplace is so connected, dialogue is so active in social networks, and search engines (both regular and blog-specific) are so well adjusted to the new LIVE nature of the Web.

    There are two types of listening and observing: active and passive.

    Active listening is like being at a party: you're interacting, you're engaged, and you're in there. Passive listening is like being behind the glass of a focus group: you're observing the market or your target audience from a distance.

    You want to practice both types of listening, as they're equally important.

6. **Thou shalt participate, comment, and converse in context.**

    Break this law and you'll get knocked down very quickly. It's easy to see why, when you think of a common offline scenario. As an analogy, let's say you're at a party or a barbeque.

You see a group of people talking and you jump in and say, "Hey, how is everybody doing today? I sell Corvettes. I just pulled up in my new Corvette. Would you like to buy a Corvette? I have a red Corvette convertible I can give you a good deal on. Would you like to buy a Corvette now?"

What's going to happen?

As you might imagine, one of two things will take place. The group will either beat the heck out of you, or they're going to tell you to take a hike.

In more polite crowds, they may not say a thing. All they'll do is subtly edge you out of the circle, leaving you standing outside, with your drink in your hand, looking all around, pretending you're not really interested in talking with that group after all.

If you enter a conversation, listen first to find out what they're talking about. See if the conversation is relevant. If you hear something that indicates they share a similar passion for fast cars, you'll have a better chance of successfully contributing.

If you really are a salesperson or own a dealership, then you would not be poking your head in and interrupting. You're coming in and getting a feel for the crowd, because you followed commandment number four above by listening and observing your target audience. Only then should you begin commenting and conversing in context. Only then will you be accepted.

You build rapport and as opportunities come up or as you get better with influence and persuasion strategies, you'll be able to guide the conversation in a customer-centric way by remembering the group's wants, needs and desires.

What are they looking for? How can you solve a problem, meet their needs, or remove pain? If you can answer these questions, you will be successful in the online networking world.

There is a right way and a wrong way to comment on other people's blogs, especially if you're going to refer them to your blog.

Contribute in context. Make sure your comment adds to the conversation in some meaningful way. In other words, don't just say, "Oh yeah, I wrote an article about that on my blog, go check it out." This is the fastest way to break rapport and ruin relationships in the online community. It's clearly seen as self-serving, and doesn't help anyone but you.

Your comment is your opportunity to prove that what you have to share is valuable – the more valuable, the more likely people are to check you out further. But, you must prove yourself first; then people will join your party. The remaining commandments are a bit more practical in terms of business blog structure and administration.

7. **Thou shalt only call it content if it's linkable.**

    If you post any type of content (written, audio, images, or video), people need to be able to reference your content on their blog. There needs to be a **permanent link for all of your content.**

    Blogging software takes care of this automatically, but what's important is that, as you create new content, it needs to be searchable, and able to be indexed and referenced.

There should be no "rotting links" like those that mass-media outlets and large corporate sites are famous for. This refers to what happens when a site posts an article then moves it to an archive. The original link changes with no auto-forwarding feature, or worse, you get a "404 error: page cannot be found."

Those are the annoying things that stop the New Media Marketplace from working properly, and it stops your credibility almost immediately.

8. **Thou shalt assume that readers will enter your site from any and every page.**

Old-school Internet thinking via the World Wide Web was: Put up a Web page, and visitors will come to your site through the home page.

If you put up a corporate Web site with many pages, people would normally come to the front page and then spider out into those other pages.

This is no longer the case because of the way that search engines' algorithms have changed, as well as the way the new World LIVE Web functions.

Your search engine rankings are going to come from the keyword-rich content on your business blog. So, when people visit your domain coming from a regular search engine, they're going to be coming in through any number of pages you have on your blog.

If you have 200 posts on your blog, people can come in through any one of those 200 pages. When they land, you have to have made adjustments to your old Web Marketing 1.0 thinking and compensate for that with your blog structure.

Emails can reference you, other blogs can reference you, and if that happens on a post that went up three weeks ago, there may have been a dozen posts since then, so they're now entering your site through the archives section.

Think about what your blog site looks like. Think about how it is structured for name capture, for taking the conversation to the next level, and for making the relationship with your readers even more personal.

9. Thou shalt encourage participation on individual pages.

Some of this is already built into the blogging software, through commenting and TrackBacks. That encourages participation, so make that prominent at the bottom of every one of your posts or articles. You can even add cool plug-ins like having a convenient button for your blog visitors to push to send your article as an email to their friends.

Not everyone is up to speed on RSS though, and not everyone understands how a blog works, so you don't want to make it difficult for people who are new to the New Media. Make it easy to generate a printer-friendly page or send an article to a friend via email.

10. Thou shalt test and track often.

Testing: Don't just assume that what you are writing about is what people are interested in – at least not the words you use. You could have done all your research correctly with your target audience. You could be talking about the right topics.

However, if the keywords you're using are not triggering anyone's interest or being used in open Internet searches, you'll catch fewer people's attention than you could if you scientifically test your results.

You can maximize buzz when you use words that your target audience uses in everyday conversation. Once again, we're right back to the importance of communicating and connecting with your audience and clients.

To get feedback, you can post popularity surveys and use different words to describe the same topic and see what people choose.

It doesn't matter if several dozen people respond to a survey like that; it's a heck of a lot better than you assuming that you know what words are good trigger words for your audience. You may know your target audience's wants, needs, and desires, but you might not be using the right trigger words.

You can test different headlines on a similar topic and then track your server logs. What headlines are drawing the most traffic in terms of your posts?

Tracking: This is one of those crossover principles that existed in Web Marketing 1.0. It's still critical for your success with Web Marketing 2.0, except now you can take your research to a whole new level with more human interaction combined with your research.

You want to monitor and track through your server logs and/or traffic analysis software. You also want to track your links when you're linking out, whether it's in a post or it's in a sidebar or a special promotion. You need to be tracking those links out of your blog back to your sales page or to your Web site and you want to know what's working.

Tracking is another way to see what words and topics are generating the most interest related to your product. All of this is to make sales, but you can't do that unless you know what's working. That's why testing and tracking is so pivotal to this process and your ultimate success.

Section IV

≫Take ACTION!

Podcasting for Profit

chapter fifteen

"You know the problem with Hollywood? They make crap, unbelievable, unremarkable crap.

Now I'm not some grungy wanna-be filmmaker that's searching for existentialism through a haze of bong smoke. It's easy to pick apart bad acting, shortsighted directing, or purely moronic stringing together of words many of the studies term as prose.

No, I'm talking about the lack of realism. Realism is not a pervasive element in the modern American cinematic vision. And realism is what people crave."

- Gabriel in the movie Swordfish

》》There's no better time to become a "Radio Star" than today.

In fact, with the popularity and success of reality TV these days, it's never been easier to become a TV Star either! Especially with the amazing tool that Podcasting brings to the average Joe.

What most people don't realize about Podcasting, is that Podcasting can either be delivered as audio on demand, or video on demand. Some have tried to define the differences by calling it V-Blogging, for video blogging.

There's even something called "Mo-Blogging" which stands for Mobile Blogging, meaning "blogging on the go" – literally. This is where you can use your mobile phone or landline in order to Podcast material while you're traveling or at a seminar.

Perhaps you see something really cool while you're walking along a city street on vacation or cutting edge right in your town and you want to share it with your viewers. Mo-Blogging makes that possible.

You simply call in from your cell phone or land line, and get your message to your viewers – in minutes! That's how easy it is!

You Too Can Be a Multimedia Super Star!

YouTube.com is becoming one of the fastest growing places where the average Ninja is becoming famous. That's because people are flocking to the Internet, in many cases, as a result of someone sending them a link to a funny or engaging video they couldn't help but share.

As a result, buzz about a person, product or brand is spreading all over the place – simply because people like to share things that are entertaining with their friends, family and network. Whether it's a favorite video or audio clip – it's getting sent to 100's of friends within seconds of watching it on the Internet. And yes, this includes actual commercials.

Yep. You heard that right – commercials are being sent from people like your closest friends or co-workers – right to your email!

I couldn't believe it either, until I started doing it myself. Today, when we were taking a break from working on this book, my partner and I pushed our notes to the side, and went to YouTube.com for a mini-comedy break.

We tuned in to one of our favorite channels, and watched the latest video Podcast from our favorite Ninja. (AskANinja.com)

While we were there laughing our butts off, we clicked on a few others. One had something to do with a funny dog, and since we're dog people, it caught our eye. So we checked it out. After all, it was only thirty seconds, and we weren't ready to go back to writing just yet.

There it was. A fully-grown, fully wrinkled Sharpe, taking a ride in a hot, red car. As the car accelerated, there was the Sharpe with his head out the window, wind rushing past him ironing out all his wrinkles. Too funny!

Just then, the driver stops, and after a little whine from the dog as all his wrinkles flopped back into place, we saw it... the Mercedes logo in the front of the car. It was a car commercial all along!

Wouldn't you know it! Here we were, saving a car commercial to our favorites, so we could have a laugh anytime we got stressed out in the future. I shared this video with my cousin on the spot.

In return she sent me the Volkswagen video from their series "Unpimp Your Ride". Here we were, grown adults, sending each other commercials over the Internet! Why? Because the commercials were disguised as comedy and they served as entertainment. So we were happy to pass it along.

That's the power of creating Buzz for your product, service or personality in the New Media marketplace. You create something your fans will appreciate, and they'll be more than happy to forward it to their ten closest friends or 100 not-so-close friends and contacts who would appreciate the video. (Or the humor break, as the case may be.)

So... what exactly is Podcasting?

In Chapter 4, we briefly introduced you to the power tool of Podcasting. Now, let's dig a little deeper so you can begin to generate ideas on how you can use Podcasting for your business, product or service.

Some have understood what Podcasting is through their understanding of Internet Radio. But Podcasting is different and comes with slight distinctions that make all the difference in the world.

Podcasting is the activity of creating time-shifted audio and uploading it to the Internet. The difference is, that as opposed to Internet Radio, Podcasting lets you take your music, video or educational content on the go using an MP3 player or iPod. And it puts the consumer in control to listen or watch the Podcast show whenever he or she wants.

Using an assortment of software and optional hardware you "record and store" audio programs on your blog. Then, you broadcast whatever you'd like over the Internet utilizing the automatic syndication power using RSS technology.

Audio and video episodes also get archived at specialized sites like YouTube.com and iTunes.com for distribution to an even wider audience.

A common and very accurate analogy for describing how a Podcast works is by using TiVo® as an example. If you're not familiar with TiVo®, it is a brand of DVR (Digital Video Recorder) that allows you to record your favorite TV programs to a hard drive, and watch them whenever it's convenient for you.

With TiVo® you don't have to worry about rushing home to watch that favorite program of yours. Just click the record button while reviewing your cable or satellite schedule and that's all you need to do.

The record indicator shows up on your schedule which tells TiVo® what you want to record and when you want to record it. Then you can watch the selected program at your leisure. Best part about it, is that you get to skip the commercials with the click of a button using your remote control.

This is what is referred to as time-shifted video. For example, instead of you having to be home to watch your favorite show at 8 p.m., your DVR or TiVo® automatically records the show at 8 p.m. while you're still at the gym, or picking up your daughter from her soccer match.

Instead of watching the program when it's aired LIVE at 8 p.m., you watch it later that night, perhaps at 10 p.m., or days later when it's most convenient for you.

A Podcast operates in the same manner from the listener or viewer's perspective, except the Podcast uses the Internet and RSS as its delivery channel.

RSS allows you to time-shift your audio or video recordings. And RSS allows for the syndication, distribution, and subscription of your audio or video content.

You can receive entertainment, commentary, updates, education and instruction, or any type of information-based communications that helps boost your personal performance, business knowledge or revenue.

If you're a business owner who has something valuable to share, this is an exciting breakthrough! Now, you get to deliver all of the above as it applies to your business.

And the politician who ignores this cultural trend does so at his peril. Tens of thousands of people are posting their own videos to YouTube.com and Video.Google.com every day. And they're watching what others have uploaded – including political rants and videos from other people.

Never before has a politician been able to be in touch with her constituents in a more personal way than through Podcasting (audio or video).

Beyond the town-hall meetings that became the trend in the last decade, Podcasting allows a politician to get her message across – face to face – to thousands – whether the voter is able to come out to join the town-hall meeting or not. It can all be accomplished through the simple use of a Web cam and video recorder using RSS and social networking sites where voters are already getting together and talking politics.

How The Podcast Process Works From The Publisher's Perspective

1. You record an audio or video program of some type. It can be anything you want to share with someone.

2. You then upload that audio or video to your Web server or blog.

3. You publish your Podcast on your own business or personal blog.

4. You promote it on Podcast and media specific directories for additional exposure. (Using sites like iTunes or YouTube.com which can be easily be put on auto-pilot.)

5. Then, you sit back in your Aeron chair with your favorite latte and smile. You've just discovered a new way to easily communicate with the masses.

New crowds of hungry prospects, voters or clients come knocking at your Podcast door and get to know you!

How The Podcast Process Works From The Consumer's Perspective

1. A person who wants new audio or video programs, searches for Podcasts and finds yours.

2. The listener subscribes to your Podcast by activating your Podcast feed in his media aggregator (like FeedDemon or iTunes.)

3. The listener sets a timer on his media aggregator that tells it how often to check for Podcast updates.

4. At the designated time interval, if you have a new Podcast, the listener's media aggregator will download your Podcast directly to his computer automatically.

5. Your Podcast file is also simultaneously synchronized to the listener's MP3 player (iPod, etc.).

The listener who is now a subscriber of your show, has time-shifted your Podcast by scheduling the time to download your Podcast and listen to it at her leisure.

The best part about this delivery method is the listener gets to decide when she wants to listen to or view your audio or video Podcast. She also gets to choose whether she wants to listen to your content in front of her desktop computer, or take it on the go, and listen/watch your show on her Video player, iPod or MP3 player while she's waiting to pick up the children from school.

This is connection and branding on multi-media steroids for sure!

A Podcast is NOT just another Audio MP3 or Video Recording

The differentiation here is RSS.

As you learned back in Section 2 of this book, RSS allows you to distribute your content widely across the Web through your RSS feeds. Plus, it allows users to subscribe to your audio or video content using the *time-shifted* model of multimedia consumption.

The consumer is in control!

And that's the biggest reason why Podcasting is quickly gaining in popularity and grabbing headlines. Podcasting can have a tremendous impact on your business by giving you another personalized channel of communication and connection with your audience. It's another high-touch, high-connection marketing tool of the New Media Marketplace.

And the coolest thing, is that it's morphing into something new with each new participant (like you) who gets involved. Even as we write this book, new ways of using blogs, Podcasts, and RSS are being created by business owners, politicians and consumers all over the world.

Innovation is the new differentiation factor for businesses and politicians in the New Media Marketplace of this generation. Podcasting is only limited by one's imagination.

Podcasting vs. Internet Radio

One of the challenges with Internet Radio is the only way you're able to listen to the songs, shows, or content, is stuck to your computer since it's coming at you live, through streaming audio or streaming video directly from the Internet.

Podcasting, on the other hand allows the consumer to listen to content away from their computer; and that's where the real power is. Podcasts can now be downloaded to everything from an MP3 player like an iPod to a mobile phone that is MP3 compatible, which is how new and innovative phones are being created.

By the time you get this book in your hands, T-Mobile will have released its new Sidekick 3 that's much more than a mobile phone. It lets you stay connected the way you want, when you want. Talk, TM (text message), IM (instant message), e-mail, or surf the Internet – it's all available to you in this little portable device. And thanks to the built-in MP3 player you get to listen to your favorite music or Podcast all from your own phone.

Sony PlayStation PS2 player even allows you to download Video Podcasts that can be viewed on the go. Apple's 60 gig iPod lets you take 1,000 hours of audio or 150 hours of video on the road. And when you fly non-stop from Hawaii to New York on a regular basis – this is extremely valuable for the business traveler who wants to take both educational content and entertaining movies on the plane to make the trip as enjoyable as possible.

The choices, control and communication channels are now in the consumer's hands – literally. The only question is how will you maximize this new communication channel for your business?

How will you get your message out to the masses?

The Bottom Line on Podcasting:

Podcasting isn't cutting edge. Right now, it's leading edge.

If you are going to base your marketing on what is happening right now with Podcasting, you'll miss out on a huge opportunity in the years to come.

There are so many different ways you can use Podcasting for your business.

Wayne Gretsky, the world famous championship hockey player from Canada can teach us a thing or two on how to dominate the playing field.

When asked by a reporter how he got to be such a great player, he answered, *"Most players skate to where the puck is. I skate to where the puck is going."*

If you want to capture the lion's share in your industry, business or niche, Podcasting will give you a huge advantage when it comes to getting face-to-face with your consumer – without them ever walking into your store.

A year from now, the playing field will be completely different from what it was a decade ago.

You just can't think about these opportunities with the mind of an adult. You need to put your curiosity hat on and think like you did as a child, absorbing new information like a sponge, and applying it as needed.

Teens are picking up on Podcasting faster than ever, because the mind of a young person is still adaptable. They haven't become creatures of habit like adults.

Most adults take a little longer to catch on to the next Revolution. Don't be like most people. Take advantage of this now, and get together with a mastermind of people who want to learn, adapt and capture their market share before your competitor is comfortable with this new communication channel.

Capture the mindshare of your ideal audience before they create their own listening and viewing habits with your competitor who puts up a Podcast before you catch on.

Even if you don't quite feel ready to start your own Podcast immediately after reading this book, you'll want to at least begin to participate as a consumer. You'll learn what to do for your own Podcast Show by watching what the most popular audio and video Podcasters are doing.

Start with iTunes.com and YouTube.com for now and expand your exposure from there.

You'll get plenty of innovative ideas for your own business by modeling the best and putting a unique spin on it, according to your own personality and topic.

Podcasting, along with business blogging and a number of other key New Media tools are proving to be invaluable components of an incredibly effective system for interactive marketing.

Are you ready for a revolutionary experience in your book reading adventures?

In the following four iChapters, you'll see, hear, and learn just how exciting and powerful New Media marketing can be for you, your business, and your profits.

≫ Introducing Chapters 16-18
The iChapters

"What is the use of a book, without pictures or conversations?"

- Alice in Wonderland

Since this book is all about the Secrets of Online Influence and Persuasion using blogs, Podcasts and other New Media Tools...we thought it would be fun to share some secrets that can <u>only be found online</u>. A practical way to introduce you to the practical power of New Media Marketing.

The following iChapters are online for you to not just passively download and read, but we invite you to **participate in the dialogue**. That's what the New Media Marketplace is all about.

These four iChapters are your opportunity to add to, expand, and become a part of this book. We get to hear from you, and you get to hear from some of the experts we interviewed while doing research for this book. We've even uploaded a few Podcasts for you in association with the following iChapters.

Now, all you need to access the pathway to superior success with your New Media Marketing is the Code.

By using the following links and passwords for each chapter we've given you on the following pages, you'll unlock the profit producing secrets held in these four iChapters.

The iChapters are about your imagination, interaction and ideas.

If you've ever seen the movie, *The NeverEnding Story*, you'll remember it's a story about a young boy named Bastian who escapes to the attic far away from everyone to read an ancient story-book which he's warned can be very dangerous. With little food and a flashlight, he is hungry and scared; but the NeverEnding Story-book keeps calling his attention.

Not realizing what he is about to do, he opens the book and begins to not only read, but to participate with the story as he creates **"The Never Ending Story"**. Bastian takes on the role of the character in the book, Atreyu. From that moment on, Bastian's thoughts and dreams become a reality in a far away world called Fantasia.

Bastian's vivid imagination takes him beyond the limits of the real world, much like your participation in the iChapters will take you beyond the limitations of the real world into the New Media Marketplace, called the Blogosphere.

You'll interact not only with the authors of this book, but with other readers as well. You'll have a voice, as you become co-authors to this never ending story of the *Secrets to Online Persuasion*.

G'mork: *Brave warrior, fight the nothing.*

Atreyu: *But I can't! I can't get beyond the boundaries of Fantasia.*

G'mork laughs. *Fantasia has no boundaries.*

It's the world of human fantasy. Every part, every creature in it, is a small piece of the hopes and dreams of mankind. Therefore, it has no boundaries.

There's a crash and more rocks fall.

Atreyu: *But then, why is Fantasia dying?*

G'mork: *Because people have begun to lose their hopes and forget their dreams. So the nothing grows stronger.*

Atreyu: *What's the nothing?!*

G'mork: *It's the emptiness that's left. It's despair, destroying this world. And I have been trying to help it.*

Atreyu: *But why?*

G'mork: *Because people who have no hopes are easy to control. And whoever has control has the power.*

~ *From the Movie,* The NeverEnding Story

»Enter The iChapters

iBuzz

chapter sixteen

>>> Creative ways to use Podcasts and other Multimedia Tools for Runaway Word-of-Mouth Marketing Impact

Link:
www.advancedbusinessblogging.com/businessblog/ibuzz/

Password: aloha16

iBrand

chapter seventeen

>> The Fingerprint of Emotion (versus the smudge marks of Mass Media)

Link:
www.advancedbusinessblogging.com/businessblog/ibrand/

Password: 4aloha17

iConnect

chapter eighteen

>> The Handshake heard around the World

Link:
www.advancedbusinessblogging.com/businessblog/iconnect/

Password: 18aloha

iProfit

chapter nineteen

>>> The Complete 360º System for Marketing with New Media

Link:
www.advancedbusinessblogging.com/businessblog/iprofit/

Password: hawaii808

Now... It's up to You.

》Take ACTION!

Ideas can change the world.

Planning is invaluable for long-term success.

*Wisdom and Understanding will give you
the edge in Innovation.*

But all fall short without you Taking ACTION.

*Taking Action is the secret ingredient
to every tool in this book.*

~ Deborah Cole Micek

Final Thoughts from Your Coaches and Authors

chapter twenty

Success or failure is often determined on the drawing board.

~ Robert J. McKain

≫The New Media Marketplace is here to stay. Blogs, Podcasts, social networks, and other technologies that connect people to communities are poised to dominate Internet over the next decade.

There are two simple reasons why.

1. The technology is easy to use when working with New Media.

There aren't a lot of moving parts with blogs. Podcasting is a snap for both the producer and the consumer. And when it comes to online business and marketing activities, what you have is a method of branding and connection with an ever-growing audience base that's easy to manage and has virtually no hard costs.

And, more importantly...

2. New Media connects people and fulfills a basic human need.

As you now know, the New Media Revolution is not being fueled by the technology. It's about people, participation, and persuasion.

The 21st-century marketplace is a new frontier. It's a place where consumers demand to be in control of the information they receive. The consumer is gaining more and more control with each passing week.

You can choose to fight the marketplace, or learn how to prosper in it.

When mass media tries to position blogs as a passing phase, as something with no power or impact, you'll want to keep things in perspective; these institutions are trying desperately to maintain the control they've had for nearly a century.

But now you know better. You know people are demanding. Today's consumer is getting used to something dramatically different than what mass media can provide. Unlike those industrial era institutions, you're smart enough to know that the marketplace always wins. You see what your customers are looking for. Now, armed with this information, you're ready to deliver what the people want.

When your competitors say they don't have time for "fads" like blogs or Podcasts, you can sit back, and quietly smile as you let them live in the past while you establish yourself as the leader in your niche.

However, if your friends, peers, and colleagues admit they simply don't understand the power and permanence of New Media tools like blogging, Podcasting, and social networks - do everything you can to bring them up to speed.

Let your friends know the New Media is not just about the cool new technology that's available; it's about people. Then encourage them to join you in mastering the marketplace of the new millennium.

It's hard to ignore a set of tools that can do so much for your business communication and marketing at such little expense. Our hope is that you've gained significant insight into the excitement as well as the practical business applications of blogs for successful communication, connection, and attraction of pre-qualified prospects.

The possibilities of using New Media to market and promote your business are only limited by your imagination. Be sure to refer to the iChapters 16 – 19 along with the special reports available for you at AdvancedBusinessBlogging.com.

The more innovative you are with the use of blogs and other New Media tools for your business, the easier it'll be to differentiate yourself from your competitors. With a concerted effort on your part, you'll have your competitors reaching for their oxygen mask while they gasp for air trying to keep up with you.

This is not Web Marketing 1.0 anymore.

With increased competition for search-engine positioning, competitive prospecting, and improved customer outreach that every business is now faced with, there would appear to be an increased complexity in strategies for online success.

But now, especially with what you saw in iChapter 19 – marketing with New Media is easier than people realize. The thing that was missing for people was a system.

Most importantly, remember that establishing relationships and building rapport with your target audience is what will make your marketing work. This dialogue is the feedback that brings greater accuracy to your business decisions and boosts your bottom line profits.

By harnessing the power of business blogging and New Media,

- You'll gain momentum.

- You'll get a huge advantage over your competitors stuck in the (mass media mindset only) past.

- You'll stop yourself from falling behind your competitors who are already using New Media to market, promote, and grow their businesses.

Now is the time to get your New Media Marketing Strategy underway. Do it by using what's presented in this book (including the four iChapters located online) and create a mastermind with other like-minded, forward thinking colleagues, or get some outside help from an experienced strategist.

As New Media Marketing experts, we're here to help with home study courses, coaching, and consulting anytime you're ready to kick it up a notch.

Enjoy the journey, and welcome to the New Media Marketplace!

YOURS IN PERSUASION AND PROFITS,

Deborah Cole and John Paul Micek

The World's Premiere New Media Marketing Coaches

C.P.B.A., C.P.V.A. (Certified Professional Behavior and Values Analyst)

PS: Blogs are just one tool in the arsenal you will build as you master the marketplace of the new millennium. The faster you get up and running, the faster you'll gain momentum over your competitors and capture the mindshare of your chosen audience.

Navigating the New Media Marketplace and developing a workable strategy on your own can be time consuming, and in this case – that time can be your enemy.

Choosing the right tools and strategies that will give you the edge in today's marketplace can be easier than you may think. As New Media Marketing experts, we're here to help with home study courses, coaching, and consulting as you need it.

Stay current with what's going on in the New Media Marketplace by becoming a regular reader/listener at: www.AdvancedBusinessBlogging.com.

And when you're ready to kick your New Media Marketing up to a whole new level, we've got the resources to help you put your 360º New Media Strategy into action – fast!

For tons of FREE New Media Marketing resources visit:

www.advancedbusinessblogging.com/newmediamarketingresources/

Why Hesitate?

≫Take ACTION Today!

Upon the plains of hesitation

are the bleached bones of countless millions,

who on the threshold of victory…

sat down to wait,

and in waiting,

they died.

~ Author Unknown
I guess he waited too long to put his name on this quote

»Acknowledgements

Without these fabulous people, you might not be holding this book in your hands, and we might not be holding our sanity in ours by now.

YOU! Our Readers! Thanks for picking up this book and APPLYING what you learn – and then – telling a friend (and referring them to our blog). We look forward to meeting you online!

Our Students of the BLOG Interactive 360™ Course! Especially for our founding members who joined our pre-launch program, working with us through our New Media Marketing trials and tribulations in order to test, measure and track what works best. **YOU ROCK!** All the Best to your blogging success!

David L. Hancock, our Publisher from Morgan James Publishing.

One of the most exciting days of creating this book was meeting David at a book author's publishing conference, and getting our book picked up by a New York Publisher distributed through Ingram! We're thrilled to begin this partnership together with you and your team, and we look forward to partnering on all the future books still bouncing around in our heads – that need to get onto paper.

The Morgan James Publishing Team, the entire **Design team** led by **Heather Kirk** and the **Administrative team** led by **Jeanette Barnes,**

Director of Author Relations. You each played a vital role in helping us make this book what it is right now – and on bookshelves everywhere. Coffee and chocolates are on their way for all those late-nights you put in for us.

Nancy James – thanks for editing the final manuscript, and making all the suggestions for necessary changes.

John William Roney, from the *Entrepreneurial Author University (EAU)*. Thanks for all the brilliant masterminding on this project with David and **Heather Kirk**. Your ideas and insight were brilliant and indispensable to this project's end result. We look forward to continuing to work with you and serving as faculty for EAU in the months to follow.

Franco our programmer and blog designer, and **Kathleen Cole,** for the amazing photography you contributed to this book, and the next book coming around the corner.

Lanita Gaul, our Office Manager for RPM Success Group® Inc. Thanks for holding down the fort while we needed to sequester ourselves to get this book finished to meet the deadline and release these secrets to the public. You are our rock!

Terry J. Hannon and Terri L. Green, our virtual transcriptionists. Thanks for flying through all the TeleClasses and Interview recordings to help us pen our words to paper, and begin the book writing journey – the best is yet to come with the continuation of this book online with the iChapters – get ready!

Carol Williams, our original manuscript editor of the Blog 360 Course. Thanks for everything you did to help us get this book ready for our students and to send out to a New York publisher. Your meticulous attention to detail has helped us help our readers – especially on such a highly technical subject – with new words and terminologies coming out every day.

Our Parents, Jonathan and Patricia Micek & Frederick and Victoria Cole for all your encouragement, support and character building that helped shape us to handle all the challenges that came our way – from our college days to our new business venture days.

Our Friends who have supported us all along our crazy journey; thanks for putting up with our travel schedule and connecting with us when we're in town. Your friendship means a lot!

Thanks for being there for us all along the way, inspiring and motivating us to pursue our dreams. Extra-special thanks to those of you who were with me via IM during those all-nighters I had to pull to get this book into the hands of our publisher and meet the publication deadline. You know who you are, and I love ya'!

Our Creator for revealing your destiny and purpose for our lives, and equipping us to see opportunities coming around the corner. We give you the glory for all the results achieved from our blogging efforts for our own business – and for enabling us to make the move to paradise on earth, and enjoy the island of Hawaii.

» About Your Authors and Coaches

Deborah Cole Micek, and her partner in business and life, **John-Paul Micek** are founders of the business performance consultancy, **RPM Success Group ® Inc**. They are the world's premiere New Media Marketing Consultants helping business owners and politicians generate real world results from their online efforts. They've combined their unique styles in coaching thousands of small-business owners around the world to combine online and offline strategies along with proven influence and persuasion techniques to boost personal fulfillment, build high performance teams and make more sales.

Official Coach for the award winning season one, *Dream Makeover Hawaii* TV show that aired on NBC and schooled in psychology and human performance, Deborah has a magnetic ability to enlighten, energize, and motivate you to reach the top of your game so you'll become the king or queen of the hill in your niche.

Her ability to Coach leaders on the effective use of body language and subconscious persuasion strategies put her on the map in the political and business arena.

When it comes to taking control of your business, and creating the lifestyle you really want, Coach John Paul brings his extensive entrepreneurial experience to the table for your rapid growth and expansion (for your business – not your mid-section).

Starting at age 12 with his first business, John-Paul has created a book of secret business systems that show you precisely how to make your business work hard for you.

After starting and growing four successful businesses, he reveals his no nonsense system to business growth. He's developed a Click-and-Mortar system with a proven track record that gives you practical "how-to" steps to guarantee your success.

His passion for politics gets him recognized by US governors and senators who realize the importance of using New Media strategies to get the edge in today's tough political climate where word-of-mouth means everything and every vote is crucial for victory.

 Together, they've partnered over the last decade to create a level of financial success in business and real estate that would equip most people to retire. But instead, John-Paul and Deborah decided to follow their passion, move 6,000 miles from the New York metropolitan area to the most remote island chain in the world – Hawaii, where they're currently living their dreams while helping other small-business owners do the same.

Personally mentored by America's top business minds with hundreds of hours of face time with leaders like Anthony Robbins, Jay Abraham, Robert Kiyosaki, and Stephen Pierce – Coaches Deborah and John-Paul now share with you the strategies and secrets that helped them reach their dreams.

Columnists for the *Honolulu Star Bulletin*, Hawaii's daily newspaper, you can find their weekly *Secrets to Success* in the Business Section every Sunday.

With powerful coaching programs, practical "how-to" products, and interactive teleseminars, they help you bridge the digital divide to gain the profits, personal fulfillment, and lifestyle you deserve.

Visit www.PowerPersuasionProfits.com to see how you can put their street-smart strategies to work for you today. Contact your coaches at books@RPMsuccess.com or toll free in the US at 888-334-8151.

Be sure to become a weekly reader of your Author's mega popular blog, and stay up to date on all the trends happening with New Media by getting a free subscription at: www.AdvancedBusinessBlogging.com.

» GRAB YOUR $297.00 GIFT — FOR FREE! «

For more money making ideas on using business blogs and other New Media tools to market and grow your business -- remember to grab your $297.00 Coaching Bonus for *FREE!!!*

Go to <u>FreeNewMediaCoaching.com</u>

(Hurry! While supplies last.)

»Additional Resources

For additional free resources, cool tools and traffic generating secrets, including a business blogging jump start package, visit:

http://www.AdvancedBusinessBlogging.com/NewMediaMarketingResources/

Check out what books your authors and Coaches recommend and continue learning more about the Secrets of Online Persuasion.

And **REMEMBER – tell a friend about this book!**

People will always remember the first person that turned them on to a cool tool or new trend in the marketplace.

Be **that person.**

www.ingramcontent.com/pod-product-compliance
Lightning Source LLC
Chambersburg PA
CBHW020727180526
45163CB00001B/135